Turn Your Radio On:

Radio Devotions – 2020

Rev. Jeff Williams

Trinity Lutheran Church

Slayton, Minnesota

Copyright

Permissions

Print edition

Scripture quotations are from the ESV®Bible (The Holy Bible, English Standard Version®), copyright © 2001 by Crossway, a publishing ministry of Good News Publishers. Used by permission. All rights reserved.

Digital edition

Scripture quotations are from the ESV®Bible (The Holy Bible, English Standard Version®), copyright © 2001 by Crossway, a publishing ministry of Good News Publishers. Used by permission. All rights reserved. May not copy or download more than 500 consecutive verses of the ESV Bible or more than one half of any book of the ESV Bible.

Copyright

Copyright ©2021 by Jeffrey B. Williams

All rights reserved. This book or any portion thereof may not be reproduced or used in any manner whatsoever without the express written permission of the publisher except for the use of brief quotations in a book review.

Printed in the United States of America

First Printing, 2021

Trinity Lutheran Church
2105 King Avenue
Slayton, MN 56172

Dedication and Acknowledgements

Dedication

This book is dedicated to the glory of God that He has allowed me the honor of bringing the good news of salvation to Slayton.

Acknowledgements

Many people have encouraged me in writing this book. Scott and Phyllis Mansch helped with proof reading and suggestions. Without the help and support of my long-suffering spouse unit, Sally, this book would not have become a reality.
    Thank you.

Introduction

In January, 2020, I accepted the call to serve as pastor of Trinity Lutheran Church, Slayton, Minnesota. We had been living in Colorado for over fifteen years, the last six serving the highest Lutheran congregation in North America in Leadville. The time had come to move, for various reasons, all doing with the negative effect of altitude.

One of the projects which I inherited when arriving in Slayton was an outreach broadcast over the local radio station, KJOE, 106.1. The pastor records a ninety second to two minute devotional which airs each weekday morning. My recordings started in March. Through the middle of September, each devotion aired for two mornings. After that, they were changed daily. The dates in the *Table of Contents* are the approximate air date.

Although I have done extensive writing, I have never written complete devotions in under 500 words. A two-hundred page book on computer networking, including course materials, no problem. A six-page sermon, double spaced, easy. A complete exposition of law and Gospel with the focus on the atoning sacrifice of Christ Jesus in less than a page, this is hard. As the sainted Doctor Donald Deffner would say in class, "I wrote you a long letter because I didn't have the time to write a short one."

I can see the evolution of the devotions in the short time from March to December, 2020. It has gotten easier to focus on one simple theme each day. When a topic warrants deeper treatment, I will use the same text for multiple mornings, but in a way that does not leave the audience in the lurch if they missed the previous day. In each devotion I have tried to proclaim the law and the Gospel. For the most part, I have succeeded, but there have been lapses.

The message the church proclaims is simple; we, who are sinful from the moment of conception, are unable to save ourselves from sin and death. Only God can redeem us and give us the hope of everlasting life. The Father sent His only-begotten Son, Jesus Christ, to live as a man in our place, to bear the burden of our sin though He is sinless. For His sake, we are forgiven. The Holy Spirit creates the faith which holds firmly to the promise of salvation. This is purely God's work, we are unable to save ourselves.

God comes to us in the means of grace, which are the proclaimed Word and the properly administered sacraments. We have the objective proof of God's desire that all people be saved and come to the knowledge of the truth.

I pray that you will find these *Moments of Meditation* helpful and enjoyable. My plan is to publish these devotions each year.

If you have questions or comments, please feel free to email me at `pastor@trinityslayton.net`.

Written this Transfiguration Sunday, January 24, 2021.

Rev. Jeff Williams

Contents

Dedication and Acknowledgements	iii
Introduction	iv
Contents	vi
03/27/2020 – *We Preach Christ Crucified* – 1 Corinthians 1:23	1
03/30/2020 – *Faith* – Hebrews 11:1	2
04/02/2020 – *Suffering* – Romans 5:1-5	3
04/06/2020 – *Why the Bible?* – John 20:30-31	5
04/08/2020 – *Preach the Word* – 2 Timothy 4:2	6
04/10/2020 – *Christ is Risen* – Romans 10:9	7
04/13/2020 – *We Confess* – Romans 10:9	8
04/15/2020 – *Dead and Alive* – Romans 6:3-4	9
04/17/2020 – *But I Am Baptized* – Romans 6:3-4	10
04/20/2020 – *Newness of Life* – Romans 6:3-4	11
04/22/2020 – *I Am the Good Shepherd* – John 10:14	12
04/24/2020 – *I Shall Not Want* – Psalm 23:1	13
04/27/2020 – *Grace Alone* – Psalm 23:1	14
04/29/2020 – *He Makes Me Lie Down in Green Pastures* – Psalm 23:2	15

05/01/2020 – *Beside Still Waters* – Psalm 23:2	16
05/04/2020 – *He Restoreth My Soul* – Psalm 23:3	17
05/06/2020 – *Paths of Righteousness* – Psalm 23:3	18
05/08/2020 – *For His Name's Sake* – Psalm 23:3	19
05/11/2020 – *Valley of the Shadow of Death* – Psalm 23:4	20
05/13/2020 – *Valley of the Shadow of Death* – Psalm 23:4	21
05/15/2020 – *A Table Prepared – The Word* – Psalm 23:5	22
05/18/2020 – *A Table Prepared – The Sacrament* – Psalm 23:5	23
05/20/2020 – *A Table Prepared – The Church* – Psalm 23:5	24
05/22/2020 – *Dwelling in the House of the Lord* – Psalm 23:6	25
05/25/2020 – *Lord, Teach Us to Pray* – Luke 11:1	26
05/27/2020 – *Rejoice Always* – 1 Thessalonians 5:16-18	27
05/29/2020 – *Now Thank We All Our God* – 1 Thessalonians 5:16-18	28
6/016/2020 – *Pray Without Ceasing* – 1 Thessalonians 5:16-18	29
06/03/2020 – *God Hears Our Prayers* – 1 Thessalonians 5:16-18	30
06/05/2020 – *Give Thanks* – 1 Thessalonians 5:16-18	31
06/08/2020 – *Our Father – Part 1* – Matthew 6:9	32
06/10/2020 – *Our Father – Part 2* – Matthew 6:9	33
06/13/2020 – *Our Father – Part 3* – Matthew 6:9	34
06/15/2020 – *Our Father – Part 4* – Matthew 6:9	35
06/17/2020 – *Our Father – Part 5* – Matthew 6:9	36
06/19/2020 – *Hallowed Be Thy Name – Part 1* – Matthew 6:9	37

06/22/2020 – *Hallowed Be Thy Name – Part 2* – Matthew 6:9 38

06/24/2020 – *Hallowed Be Thy Name – Part 3* – Matthew 6:9 39

06/26/2020 – *Thy Kingdom Come – Part 1* – Matthew 6:10 40

06/29/2020 – *Thy Kingdom Come – Part 2* – Matthew 6:10 41

07/01/2020 – *Thy Will Be Done – Part 1* – Matthew 6:10 42

07/03/2020 – *Thy Will Be Done – Part 2* – Matthew 6:10 43

07/06/2020 – *Thy Will Be Done – Part 3* – Matthew 6:10 44

07/08/2020 – *Give Us This Day Our Daily Bread – Part 1* – Matthew 6:11 45

07/10/2020 – *Give Us This Day Our Daily Bread – Part 2* – Matthew 6:11 46

07/13/2020 – *Give Us This Day Our Daily Bread – Part 3* – Matthew 6:11 47

07/15/2020 – *Forgive Us Our Trespasses – Part 1* – Matthew 6:12 48

07/17/2020 – *Forgive Us Our Trespasses – Part 2* – Matthew 6:12 49

07/20/2020 – *Forgive Us Our Trespasses – Part 3* – Matthew 6:12 50

07/22/2020 – *Forgive Us Our Trespasses – Part 5* – Matthew 6:12 51

07/24/2020 – *Lead Us Not Into Temptation – Part 1* – Matthew 6:13 52

07/27/2020 – *Lead Us Not Into Temptation – Part 2* – Matthew 6:13 53

07/29/2020 – *Lead Us Not Into Temptation – Part 3* – Matthew 6:13 54

07/31/2020 – *Lead Us Not Into Temptation – Part 4* – Matthew 6:13 55

08/03/2020 – *Lead Us Not Into Temptation – Part 5* – Matthew 6:13 56

08/05/2020 – *But Deliver Us From Evil – Part 1* – Matthew 6:13 57

08/07/2020 – *But Deliver Us From Evil – Part 2* – Matthew 6:13 58

08/10/2020 – *But Deliver Us From Evil – Part 3* – Matthew 6:13	59
08/12/2020 – *For Thine is the Kingdom* – Matthew 6:13	60
08/14/2020 – *Amen* – Matthew 6:13	61
08/17/2020 – *With the Lord Begin Your Task – Part 1* – Colossians 3:17	62
08/19/2020 – *With the Lord Begin Your Task – Part 2* – Colossians 3:17	63
08/21/2020 – *With the Lord Begin Your Task – Part 3* – Colossians 3:17	64
08/24/2020 – *With the Lord Begin Your Task – Part 4* – Colossians 3:17	65
08/26/2020 – *With the Lord Begin Your Task – Part 5* – Colossians 3:17	66
08/28/2020 – *Seek First – Part 1* – Matthew 6:33	67
08/31/2020 – *Seek First – Part 2* – Matthew 6:33	68
09/02/2020 – *Seek First – Part 3* – Matthew 6:33	69
09/04/2020 – *Seek First – Part 4* – Matthew 6:33	70
09/07/2020 – *Seek First – Part 5* – Matthew 6:33	71
09/09/2020 – *Blessed are the Poor in Spirit – Part 1* – Matthew 5:3	72
09/11/2020 – *Blessed are the Poor in Spirit – Part 2* – Matthew 5:3	73
09/14/2020 – *Blessed are They that Mourn, for They Shall be Comforted – Part 1* – Matthew 5:4	74
09/16/2020 – *Blessed are They that Mourn, for They Shall be Comforted – Part 2* – Matthew 5:4	75
09/18/2020 – *Blessed are the Meek – Part 1* – Matthew 5:5	76

09/21/2020 – *Blessed are the Meek – Part 2* – Matthew 5:5   77

09/22/2020 – *Blessed are Those Who Hunger and Thirst – Part 1* – Matthew 5:6   78

09/23/2020 – *Blessed are Those Who Hunger and Thirst – Part 2* – Matthew 5:6   79

09/24/2020 – *Blessed are the Merciful – Part 1* – Matthew 5:7   80

09/25/2020 – *Blessed are the Merciful – Part 2* – Matthew 5:7   81

09/28/2020 – *Blessed are the Merciful – Part 3* – Matthew 5:7   82

09/29/2020 – *Blessed are the Merciful – Part 4* – Matthew 5:7   83

09/30/2020 – *Blessed are the Pure in Heart – Part 1* – Matthew 5:8   84

10/01/2020 – *Blessed are the Pure in Heart – Part 1* – Matthew 5:8   85

10/02/2020 – *Blessed are the Peacemakers* – Matthew 5:9   86

10/05/2020 – *Blessed are the Persecuted – Part 1* – Matthew 5:10   87

10/06/2020 – *Blessed are the Persecuted – Part 2* – Matthew 5:10   88

10/07/2020 – *Blessed are the Persecuted – Part 3* – Matthew 5:10   89

10/08/2020 – *Blessed are You When Persecuted – Part 1* – Matthew 5:11-12   90

10/09/2020 – *Blessed are You When Persecuted – Part 2* – Matthew 5:11-12   91

10/12/2020 – *Law and Gospel* – Romans 8:3-4   92

10/13/2020 – *The First Use – Part 1* – Luke 10:27   93

10/14/2020 – *The First Use – Part 2* – 1 Timothy 1:9-10   94

10/15/2020 – *The Second Use – Part 1* – 1 John 1:10   95

10/16/2020 – *The Second Use – Part 2* – 1 John 1:10   96

10/19/2020 – *The Third Use* – Proverbs 6:23	97
10/03/2020 – *No Other Gods – Part 1* – Exodus 20:3	98
10/21/2020 – *No Other Gods – Part 2* – Exodus 20:3	99
10/22/2020 – *No Other Gods – Part 3* – Exodus 20:3	100
10/23/2020 – *Graven Images* – Exodus 20:4-6	101
10/26/2020 – *Name of God – Part 1* – Exodus 20:7	103
10/27/2020 – *Name of God – Part 2* – Exodus 20:7	104
10/28/2020 – *Name of God – Part 3* – Exodus 20:7	105
10/29/2020 – *Sabbath Day – Part 1* – Exodus 20:8	106
10/30/2020 – *Sabbath Day – Part 2* – Exodus 20:8	107
11/02/2020 – *Sabbath Day – Part 3* – Exodus 20:8	108
11/03/2020 – *Sabbath Day – Part 4* – Exodus 20:8	109
11/04/2020 – *Honor – Part 1* – Exodus 20:12	110
11/05/2020 – *Honor – Part 2* – Exodus 20:12	111
11/06/2020 – *Honor – Part 3* – Exodus 20:12	112
11/09/2020 – *Honor – Part 4* – Exodus 20:12	113
11/10/2020 – *Honor – Part 5* – Exodus 20:12	114
11/11/2020 – *Murder – Part 1* – Exodus 20:13	115
11/12/2020 – *Murder – Part 2* – Exodus 20:13	116
11/13/2020 – *Adultery – Part 1* – Exodus 20:14	117
11/16/2020 – *Adultery – Part 2* – Exodus 20:14	118
11/17/2020 – *Property – Part 1* – Exodus 20:15	119

11/18/2020 – *Property – Part 2* – Exodus 20:15	120
11/19/2020 – *Property – Part 3* – Exodus 20:15	121
11/20/2020 – *Property – Part 4* – Exodus 20:15	122
11/23/2020 – *Property – Part 5* – Exodus 20:15	123
11/24/2020 – *Reputation – Part 1* – Exodus 20:16	124
11/25/2020 – *Reputation – Part 2* – Exodus 20:16	125
11/26/2020 – *Thanksgiving* – 1 Timothy 2:1-4	126
11/27/2020 – *Reputation – Part 3* – Exodus 20:16	128
11/30/2020 – *Reputation – Part 4* – Exodus 20:16	129
12/01/2020 – *Reputation – Part 5* – Exodus 20:16	130
12/02/2020 – *Covet – Part 1* – Exodus 20:17	131
12/03/2020 – *Covet – Part 2* – Exodus 20:17	132
12/04/2020 – *Close of the Commandments – Part 1* – Exodus 20:5b-6	133
12/07/2020 – *Close of the Commandments – Part 2* – Romans 13:3-4	134
12/08/2020 – *Close of the Commandments – Part 3* – Romans 3:20	135
12/09/2020 – *Close of the Commandments – Part 4* – Psalm 119:105	136
12/10/2020 – *Close of the Commandments – Part 5* – Psalm 119:105	137
12/11/2020 – *The Christmas Story – Part 1* – Luke 2:1-3	138
12/14/2020 – *The Christmas Story – Part 2* – Luke 2:1-3	139
12/15/2020 – *The Christmas Story – Part 3* – Luke 2:4-5	140
12/16/2020 – *The Christmas Story – Part 4* – Luke 2:4-5	141
12/17/2020 – *The Christmas Story – Part 5* – Luke 2:6-7	142

12/18/2020 – *The Christmas Story – Part 6* – Luke 2:8	143
12/21/2020 – *The Christmas Story – Part 7* – Luke 2:9	144
12/22/2020 – *The Christmas Story – Part 8* – Luke 2:10-12	145
12/23/2020 – *The Christmas Story – Part 9* – Luke 2:13-14	146
12/24/2020 – *The Christmas Story – Part 10* – Luke 2:13-14	147
12/25/2020 – *The Christmas Story – Part 11* – Luke 2:13-14	148
12/28/2020 – *The Christmas Story – Part 12* – Luke 2:15	149
12/29/2020 – *The Christmas Story – Part 13* – Luke 2:16	150
12/30/2020 – *The Christmas Story – Part 14* – Luke 2:17	151
12/31/2020 – *The Christmas Story – Part 15* – Luke 2:18-20	152
01/01/2021 – *The Christmas Story – Part 16* – Luke 2:11	153
Index	154

03/27/2020 – *We Preach Christ Crucified* – 1 Corinthians 1:23

1 Corinthians 1:23

> 23 But we preach Christ crucified, a stumbling block to Jews and folly to Gentiles (ESV)

Saint Paul, writing to the church in Corinth, said, "We preach Christ crucified." This statement sums up the entire doctrine of the Christian Church. From this statement flows the questions, "Who is Christ?" "Why was He crucified?" "What does this mean for today?" We can spend a lifetime studying this statement and still not exhaust the lessons we can learn.

Who is Christ? We believe, teach, and confess He is the Son of God, conceived by the Holy Spirit and the virgin Mary. Having no human father, He is sinless, just as Adam was sinless on the day he was created.

Why was He crucified? Unlike Jesus, we were conceived in sin, and we daily sin. Indeed, we cannot, by our own strength, overcome this sin which separates us from God. Only one who is sinless, only Jesus Christ, can reconcile us to the Father. Thus, He was crucified to bear the price of our sin.

What does this mean for today? We have the forgiveness of our sins. Because we are forgiven, we know that we have eternal life with our heavenly Father. This forgiveness is a gift, something we do not and cannot earn.

When we say, with Paul, "we preach Christ crucified," we are confessing that Jesus died and rose again to free us from sin, death, and the power of the devil.

03/30/2020 – *Faith* – Hebrews 11:1

Hebrews 11:1

> 1 Now faith is the assurance of things hoped for, the conviction of things not seen. (ESV)

The writer of Hebrews says, "Now faith is the assurance of things hoped for, the conviction of things not seen." Is faith the blind belief in something which has no proof, or is there something more?

Faith is made up of three parts. The first is knowledge. All faith is built on something we know, which is why we continue to study not only the Bible, but the world around us.

The second part is agreement. As we study, we compare new information to that which we already know to see if it fits our understanding of the world. When we are looking at something which cannot be reproduced, an historical fact, we determine if the source is trustworthy. If the source is trustworthy, we can trust the new information.

Finally, faith requires trust. All knowledge is worthless if we do not trust that which we know. Trust allows us to use our knowledge for our benefit.

We understand that our hope of everlasting life is based on faith in Jesus Christ. We know of God's plan for redeeming sinners as revealed in the Bible. We agree the Bible is an accurate source which agrees with verifiable science. We trust that Jesus was crucified, and that the tomb is empty, as the Bible claims. We have faith that Jesus died to redeem us from sin, death, and the power of the devil.

May God grant you faith in His Word, that you have life eternal in Christ Jesus.

04/02/2020 – *Suffering* – Romans 5:1–5

Romans 5:1–5

> 1 Therefore, since we have been justified by faith, we have peace with God through our Lord Jesus Christ.
>
> 2 Through him we have also obtained access by faith into this grace in which we stand, and we rejoice in hope of the glory of God.
>
> 3 More than that, we rejoice in our sufferings, knowing that suffering produces endurance,
>
> 4 and endurance produces character, and character produces hope,
>
> 5 and hope does not put us to shame, because God's love has been poured into our hearts through the Holy Spirit who has been given to us. (ESV)

Saint Paul reminded the Christians in Rome of the blessings of faith in Christ Jesus. Because we have the gift of salvation by God's rich grace and love, we have the peace which comes from knowing God is in control of everything. We see the big picture, that we do have everlasting life with our heavenly Father because of the redemption earned for us on the cross of Calvary.

He wrote:

> Therefore, since we have been justified by faith, we have peace with God through our Lord Jesus Christ. Through him we have also obtained access by faith into this grace in which we stand, and we rejoice in hope of the glory of God. More than that, we rejoice in our sufferings, knowing that suffering produces endurance, and endurance produces character, and character produces hope, and hope does not put us to shame, because God's love has been poured into our hearts through the Holy Spirit who has been given to us.

It seems strange that Christians rejoice in suffering, but we are convinced that through suffering we are drawn closer to God. Suffering also gives us a chance to help others, to have compassion on them. Even if we are home-bound, we pray that God gives His peace and comfort to our neighbors.

May you find comfort in Paul's words as you deal with the changes and chances of this world.

04/06/2020 – *Why the Bible?* – John 20:30–31

John 20:30–31

> 30 Now Jesus did many other signs in the presence of the disciples, which are not written in this book;
>
> 31 but these are written so that you may believe that Jesus is the Christ, the Son of God, and that by believing you may have life in his name. (ESV)

We have been talking about faith. Faith, which is knowlege, agreement, and trust, requires that we know that in which we believe.

Conservative Christians contend that the Bible is the inspired Word of God, that it is the truth of all we believe about God. Time and again people have attacked the Bible, but in the end it has been shown as accurate in historical details, and internally consistent.

Is the Bible just a set of rules? The guidelines given in the Bible tend to make our lives easier. Acknowledging God means that we have a perspective to handle suffering and tragedy. Honoring authority, life, marriage, property, and reputation means we live in harmony with our neighbors.

Saint John tells us about both the limits and the purpose of the Bible:

> Now Jesus did many other signs in the presence of the disciples, which are not written in this book; but these are written so that you may believe that Jesus is the Christ, the Son of God, and that by believing you may have life in his name.

The Bible is about Jesus Christ, from beginning to end, Old Testament and New. Therefore, it is about His redeeming work on the cross which brings to us life and salvation.

May our Lord comfort you with His Word, giving you the peace which comes from trusting in Christ Jesus.

04/08/2020 – *Preach the Word* – 2 Timothy 4:2

2 Timothy 4:2

> 2 Preach the word; be ready in season and out of season; reprove, rebuke, and exhort, with complete patience and teaching. (ESV)

We all have had to make changes due to the corona virus. Many businesses have been closed to help stop the spread of the disease, many people have lost steady income while furloughed.

Churches are closed, which makes the job of a pastor much harder. Saint Paul wrote to Timothy, "Preach the word; be ready in season and out of season; reprove, rebuke, and exhort, with complete patience and teaching." That is the primary duty of a pastor, the primary duty of the church.

The Word which we preach is both the Law, which reproves sin and rebukes sinners; and it is the Gospel, which exhorts and encourages us to hold firmly to the promises of God. Properly preached, we see our need for a savior from sin, death, and the power of the devil. We see how God loved the world so much that He sacrificed His only-begotten Son to give us eternal life.

Our prayers are for our leaders, for those in health-care, in public service, and all who are affected by this epidemic.

In the mean time, we look forward to the opportunity to return to church. As we honor the request that we limit public gatherings, we long for the ability to hear God's Word, and to receive His blessings.

Though Church is out of season, we are finding new ways to preach the word, to bring the message of hope in these troubled times. We continue to preach Christ crucified to redeem us from eternal death, to give us everlasting life.

May God grant you His rich blessings, especially the opportunity to hear of His Son.

04/10/2020 – *Christ is Risen* – Romans 10:9

Romans 10:9

> 9 because, if you confess with your mouth that Jesus is Lord and believe in your heart that God raised him from the dead, you will be saved. (ESV)

The church sign, one Easter morning, proclaimed, "He has risen." This is most certainly true, for Jesus rose from the dead, burst forth from the sealed tomb, and appeared to over 500 people in the forty days from Easter to the Ascension. Certainly the Bible proclaims this historical fact, as do several other sources, both secular and religious, contemporary with the early church.

We know that, if Jesus' mortal remains were found, everything about Christianity would be proven false. No matter how hard both the chief priests and the Roman government tried, they could not produce the body of the crucified Christ. People tried then, and they are still trying, to disprove this fact. So far they have failed.

Jesus Christ not only has risen from the dead, as an historical fact, He is risen from the dead, in the present tense. He is present with His church through the proclaimed Gospel and the sacraments. Though hidden from our sight, we believe, teach, and confess that it is not simply the teachings which remain, but He is truly present.

As the God who is present, though unseen, He hears our prayers, He causes His Word to be spoken for our comfort, He grants us the peace of knowing our sins are forgiven for His sake.

Therefore we are bold to proclaim, Christ is risen, He is risen indeed. Amen.

04/13/2020 – *We Confess* – Romans 10:9

Romans 10:9

> 9 because, if you confess with your mouth that Jesus is Lord and believe in your heart that God raised him from the dead, you will be saved. (ESV)

Saint Paul wrote to the church in Rome: "if you confess with your mouth that Jesus is Lord and believe in your heart that God raised him from the dead, you will be saved." He also wrote to the church in Corinth, "we preach Christ crucified,"[1] 1 Corinthians 1:23 which means the story isn't finished on Good Friday. We preach that indeed Jesus died to bear the price of our sin, and He rose again destroying the power of death.

The Christian Church confesses Jesus. By the very nature of our faith, we are compelled to share the truth of the Gospel.

That which we believe, teach, and confess is public knowledge. With our lips we confess that Jesus Christ, true God and true man, was crucified for us, is risen from the dead, and is with His church even now. Our God is not simply a myth. His story does not begin, "In a galaxy far far away," but was incarnate at a specific time, during the reign of Caesar Augustus, and a specific place, Bethlehem.

We believe the eyewitness accounts, not only is the tomb empty, but Jesus appeared to His apostles, to Paul, and to over 500 believers after His resurrection. This is not a fairy tale, this is not mass hallucination, but an historical fact.

Our loving God, working through the power of the Holy Spirit, gives us the faith to hold firmly to the promise of eternal life for the sake of Jesus Christ. We confess that Jesus is the incarnate Son of God, and that He is risen. This is most certainly true.

God grant you His peace, now and forevermore.

---

[1] 1 Corinthians 1:23 (ESV)

04/15/2020 – *Dead and Alive* – Romans 6:3–4

Romans 6:3–4

> 3 Do you not know that all of us who have been baptized into Christ Jesus were baptized into his death?
>
> 4 We were buried therefore with him by baptism into death, in order that, just as Christ was raised from the dead by the glory of the Father, we too might walk in newness of life. (ESV)

During this Easter season we are continually reminded that Christ Jesus is risen from the dead. The question arises - how does that affect us as we are dealing with all that life is throwing at us?

Jesus' resurrection, according to Saint Paul, is something that is true not only for Him, but for us. Paul wrote:

> Do you not know that all of us who have been baptized into Christ Jesus were baptized into his death? We were buried therefore with him by baptism into death, in order that, just as Christ was raised from the dead by the glory of the Father, we too might walk in newness of life.

We believe, teach, and confess that Paul is calling baptism God's work which applies the death and resurrection of Jesus to each believer. Because we are by nature sinful and unclean, we will suffer physical death. Being joined to Jesus Christ through baptism, we hold firmly to the promise of everlasting life. Our sinful human nature was drowned, and we were given, through baptism, a new life in Christ Jesus.

As believers in Jesus Christ, we believe that we are forgiven, that He has borne the guilt of our sin. We hold to our baptism as the means by which we were buried with Jesus only to rise with Him. This truth puts our lives into perspective. This truth gives us hope in times of fear and uncertainty. This truth gives us the proof of God's rich love and mercy, the hope of life everlasting.

04/17/2020 – *But I Am Baptized* – Romans 6:3–4

Romans 6:3–4

> 3 Do you not know that all of us who have been baptized into Christ Jesus were baptized into his death?
>
> 4 We were buried therefore with him by baptism into death, in order that, just as Christ was raised from the dead by the glory of the Father, we too might walk in newness of life. (ESV)

Jesus, who rose from the dead, still lives for us as our redeemer from sin and death. That He is risen from the dead is not simply an historical fact, but the ongoing truth that He is present in His church, that He is present with us.

In the same way, our baptism is not simply an historical fact, but something from which we can draw comfort each day. Martin Luther explained this in the *Large Catechism:*

> Thus we must regard Baptism and make it profitable to ourselves, that when our sins and conscience oppress us, we strengthen ourselves and take comfort and say: Nevertheless I am baptized; but if I am baptized, it is promised me that I shall be saved and have eternal life, both in soul and body.[2]

We daily return to our baptism, not as something from our past, but the assurance that we have the forgiveness of sins. By repenting our sins, we hold firmly to God's promise of forgiveness through Christ Jesus. For us, then, our baptism is a living, present act of God which brings to us faith, forgiveness, and eternal life.

May God grant you His peace, that you have life in His name.

---

[2] http://bookofconcord.org/lc-6-baptismhp

04/20/2020 – *Newness of Life* – Romans 6:3-4

Romans 6:3-4

> 3 Do you not know that all of us who have been baptized into Christ Jesus were baptized into his death?
>
> 4 We were buried therefore with him by baptism into death, in order that, just as Christ was raised from the dead by the glory of the Father, we too might walk in newness of life. (ESV)

Saint Paul reminded the Christians in Rome that we are buried with Christ through baptism so that we walk in the newness of life. What is this newness of life? Is it the constant reminder that we have failed to properly serve God and neighbor, a fear that we are not good enough to go to heaven? Or is it a true turning of our lives to God, trusting in Him for the forgiveness of our sins?

To be alive is to walk, to be raised to life is to be enabled to walk, to show all the evidence of being alive. Remaining in sin is to be without spiritual life, without spiritual activity of any kind.

Life, which is both physical and spiritual, is invisible. Our actions witness that we are alive. As ones alive in Christ, we are able to pray, to hold to Him, to confess that His death was for our redemption. As ones alive in Christ, we desire to serve Him in the same way He served us, by caring for our neighbors.

May God grant us this new life in Christ, that we may walk as ones baptized and alive in Him.

04/22/2020 – *I Am the Good Shepherd* – John 10:14

John 10:14

14 I am the good shepherd. I know my own, and my own know me. (ESV)

There are two passages in the Bible of which most people are aware. The first is John 3:16: "For God so loved the world, that he gave his only begotten Son, that whosoever believeth in him should not perish, but have everlasting life." John 3:16 The other is Psalm 23, "The LORD is my shepherd." Psalms 23:1 Christians and non-Christians alike have heard these two passages and have come to recognize them.

What does it mean that Jesus calls Himself the Good Shepherd, as John recorded in his Gospel. "I am the good shepherd. I know my own, and my own know me." We can go back to Psalm 23 and compare David's words to the actions of Jesus Christ.

In these hectic, fear-filled days, it is good to reflect on Jesus' love for His people, His precious flock. He calms us with His love, and assures us of our salvation. He has taken upon Himself our sin, and in turn, has credited us with His righteousness. He truly has restored our soul, paying the price of our sin upon the cross of Calvary.

Therefore, we are confident, even in the face of death, that the Good Shepherd is with us, guides us, and cares for us. Though we may walk through the dark shadows of the valley, He brings us the comfort of His presence through the properly proclaimed Gospel and the Sacraments He has given the Church.

We can be content, assured of the love our Shepherd gives. For His sake, because of His grace and mercy, we have the gift of everlasting life. May the Shepherd bring you this comfort in these trying times.

Amen.

04/24/2020 – *I Shall Not Want* – Psalms 23:1

Psalms 23:1

1 The LORD is my shepherd; I shall not want.

Saint Augustine, one of the early Church Fathers who died in 430 AD, wrote, "When you say, 'The LORD is my shepherd,' no proper grounds are left for you to trust in yourself."[3]

In this confession of complete reliance on God for everything we need in this life and the next, we admit that by ourselves we are unable to work our own salvation. As God works through means, He gives us our daily bread, but He also gives us the forgiveness of sins for the sake of the death and resurrection of Jesus Christ.

All we have is a gift from God, even that for which we labor. For God allows us to work, and blesses this land with produce, and causes us to work together to process, transport, and sell that which we need. The physical blessings He provides we call the "First Article gifts," confessing that "I believe in God, the Father Almighty, maker of heaven and earth."

Over the next weeks we will look at the twenty-third Psalm to better understand God's love and grace towards us. May He grant you rich blessings, today and always. Amen.

---

[3] Blaising, C. A. and Hardin, C. S., eds. (2008). *Ancient Christian commentary on scripture*, Old Testament VII: Psalms 1-50. Downers Grove, IL: IVP Academic, p. 178.

04/27/2020 – *Grace Alone* – Psalms 23:1

Psalms 23:1

1 The LORD is my shepherd; I shall not want.

We are dependent on God's rich grace and mercy. Nowhere is this more evident than as we look at our sinful condition, at our ability to pay for the things we have done against both God and neighbor. Both our actions and motives are suspect, even as we selfishly seek our own advantage.

All sin stems from Adam and his desire to be like God, knowing good and evil. Our sins against God and each other arise from our desire to be first, to be in charge, to have god-like power.

Martin Luther, the great Reformation theologian, wrote, "I believe that I cannot, by my own reason or strength, believe in my Lord Jesus Christ or come to Him."

Our Shepherd calls us to Himself, cares for us, cleanses us from our guilt, and gives us the promise of everlasting life. We can't save ourselves, but for the sake of the suffering, death, and resurrection of Jesus Christ, we can hold firmly to God's promises.

Therefore we have peace with God. We know the outcome; life in heaven with the Good Shepherd. This helps us keep the changes and chances of this world in perspective, giving us the resiliency to continue to love God and serve our neighbors.

God grant you peace in these hectic days, that our Lord is indeed our shepherd. Amen.

04/29/2020 – *He Makes Me Lie Down in Green Pastures* – Psalms 23:2

Psalms 23:2

> 2 He maketh me to lie down in green pastures: he leadeth me beside the still waters.

The Psalmist wrote, "Oh, taste and see that the LORD is good! Blessed is the man who takes refuge in him!"[4] Psalms 34:8 This fits beautifully with David's words about our Good Shepherd.

The Shepherd makes me lie down in green pastures. Physically, God provides for our daily needs, working through the means of our labor, with the help of many others in our community. Certainly the green pastures are the abundant blessings of food, shelter, and clothing which He gives.

More importantly, the green pastures are the Word of God, the ability to learn and know of His grace. These pastures are not some scrub land with bitter plants, but the lushest of grass, the best of nourishment. God's Word is true. It brings to us life everlasting, for only in God's Word do we know of His grace, His undeserved love. Only in God's Word are we told that the Father sent His Son to redeem us from sin, death, and the power of the devil.

The green pastures allow us to relax, to take the time to learn, to remember the blessings of body and soul which are ours for the sake of Christ Jesus. May our Lord grant you green pastures, food for your soul, and the peace of knowing your sins are forgiven for Christ's sake. Amen.

---

[4] Psalms 34:8 (ESV)

05/01/2020 – *Beside Still Waters* – Psalms 23:2

Psalms 23:2

> 2 He maketh me to lie down in green pastures: he leadeth me beside the still waters.

King David, himself a shepherd, looked at all the blessings of God through the eyes of a sheep. He wrote, "He leadeth me beside the still waters."

We believe, teach, and confess that the entire Bible, both Old and New Testaments, speak of Christ Jesus. When a Christian hears of water, he immediately recalls baptism, what Saint Paul called the "washing of regeneration and renewal." The still waters of baptism bring us peace, for through these waters we are brought into a relationship with God.

We are brought to the green pastures and the still waters as we come into the Church, the gathering of God's people who receive His good gifts of forgiveness, life everlasting, and the peace of being reconciled with the Father. For the Church is God's work, the place He prepared for those who have faith that Jesus Christ is the savior from sin and death. He built the Church with His hands, using the words of the prophets and evangelists to bring us the good news of salvation by grace through faith for the sake of Christ.

There, by the waters of baptism, each Christian is fed the good news of God's rich love. Thereby we have the peace which passes all understanding, the sure and certain hope of life everlasting.

May our Lord continue to lead you to the green pastures and still waters which refresh your soul, for the sake of Christ Jesus, our Lord. Amen.

05/04/2020 – *He Restoreth My Soul* – Psalms 23:3

Psalms 23:3

> 3 He restores my soul. He leads me in paths of righteousness for his name's sake. (ESV)

We have been looking at the Twenty-third Psalm. Throughout the Psalm we find that the sheep do nothing to receive the care from the Shepherd. It is the Shepherd who brings the sheep to the pastures and still water. It is the Shepherd who restores the soul.

We believe, teach, and confess that we are by nature sinful and unclean, that without the grace of God we are eternally condemned. The sin which is passed from father to child condemns us to death, both physically and spiritually. Only God, calling us with the Good News of salvation through the suffering, death, and resurrection of Jesus Christ, can give us the hope of redemption from the guilt of sin.

One of the first Lutheran hymns says:

```
    Since Christ has full atonement made
And brought to us salvation,
Each Christian therefore may be glad
And build on this foundation.
Your grace alone, dear Lord, I plead,
Your death is now my life indeed,
For You have paid my ransom.\footnote
{
LSB 555, \textit{Salvation Unto Us Has Come,} vs. 6
}
```

May God comfort you with His grace, that He has restored your soul through the forgiveness of sins. Amen.

05/06/2020 – *Paths of Righteousness* – Psalms 23:3

Psalms 23:3

> 3 He restores my soul. He leads me in paths of righteousness for his name's sake. (ESV)

What does it mean to walk in the paths of righteousness? God has restored our souls, forgiven our sins, and reconciled us to Himself through Jesus' death and resurrection. We get to respond to God's love.

Luther said, "God does not need our good works, but our neighbor does."[5] One of our post-Communion prayers asks that God use the Sacrament to "strengthen our faith towards [Him] and fervent love for one another."

This really sums up the idea of walking the paths of righteousness. God first serves us by granting us the remission of our sins. We respond by doing those things which reflect His love, helping our neighbors, giving to others that which we have received.

The parable of the Sheep and the Goats, found in Matthew's Gospel, speaks of our good works. The sheep, who are credited with feeding the hungry, clothing the naked, and a host of other works, are dumbfounded. They do not remember doing the good works. Indeed, the good works flow naturally in their lives, something accomplished without thought or remembrance. It is just what the sheep of the Good Shepherd do.

So these sheeply good works do not earn us salvation, but do show that our faith is living. These are not offerings to God, but are His works which we are privileged to do on His behalf.

May our Lord be with you as you respond in faith by showing love to one another, for the sake of Jesus Christ, our Lord. Amen.

---

[5]This may be a spurious quote which actually sums up Luther's doctrine of vocation. It is found in Wingren, G. (1957) *Luther on Vocation*. Philadelphia: Muhlenberg Press, reprinted by CPH, p. 10.

Also quoted in Veith, G. E. (2016) *Working for our neighbor*, p. 13

05/08/2020 – *For His Name's Sake* – Psalms 23:3

Psalms 23:3

> 3 He restores my soul. He leads me in paths of righteousness for his name's sake. (ESV)

As we continue looking at the Twenty-third Psalm, we come to realize that, as the sheep belonging to the Good Shepherd, we are fully dependent on Him. He calls us into His presence, enlightens us with the gifts given through the Word and Sacraments, and gives us the opportunity to respond to His love. What is the result of the Shepherd's actions?

Because we confess that we are powerless to please God by our own works, that we are selfish, even in the civil good works we might do, we deserve none of the glory. Just like the winning quarterback does not bask in the limelight, but credits the entire team with the victory, so the Christian defers the praise to God.

The name of God reveals who He is. He told Moses His name: "I am."[6] Exodus 3:13 while Isaiah called Him, "Wonderful Counselor, Mighty God, Everlasting Father, Prince of Peace."[7] Isaiah 9:6

When we give the glory to God, when we confess that it is by His grace that we are saved and that we serve our neighbors, we are simply proclaiming who He is. God is good, gracious, merciful, and kind. He desires that all people come to Him to be redeemed from sin, death, and the power of the devil. Therefore, we are led down the paths of righteousness, receiving redemption from God and serving our neighbors, to proclaim His goodness.

God grant you His grace and mercy, for His name's sake. Amen.

---

[6] Exodus 3:13
[7] Isaiah 9:6b (ESV)

05/11/2020 – *Valley of the Shadow of Death* – Psalms 23:4

Psalms 23:4

> 4 Even though I walk through the valley of the shadow of death, I will fear no evil, for you are with me; your rod and your staff, they comfort me. (ESV)

Over the years, emergency services chaplaincy has changed. In the 1980s, the chaplains were involved with responding to critical incidents, applying spiritual care after a major incident.

Today, however, many emergency service chaplains stress personal resiliency, preparing beforehand to handle the realities of life. As we still are isolated during the pandemic, we are well able to see how those who were prepared are much better off than those who react after the fact. This is true with physical supplies, food, cleaning materials, toilet paper. This is true spiritually.

The Gospel, the good news that we have eternal life for the sake of the death and resurrection of Jesus Christ, puts our suffering into perspective. Although we are declared righteous and holy in God's sight, we also live with the effects of sin. Destruction, disease, and death are the results of our rebellion against God. These realities will remain until Christ Jesus comes again to judge the living and the dead.

As Christians, we can put the effects of sin into perspective. We know there is an end to our suffering. We know that our Good Shepherd is leading us on the path which ends with life everlasting. This pandemic, the destruction by fire or water, and all the other ills, are temporary.

May God's grace and mercy grant you resiliency and comfort in these difficult days. Amen.

05/13/2020 – *Valley of the Shadow of Death* – Psalms 23:4

Psalms 23:4

> 4 Even though I walk through the valley of the shadow of death, I will fear no evil, for you are with me; your rod and your staff, they comfort me. (ESV)

President Franklin Roosevelt said, "We have nothing to fear except fear itself." As we focus on the distressing news of the current pandemic, we certainly can be left with little hope.

Origen, a second-century Church Father, wrote some sage advice for our consideration:

> To walk in the midst of the shadow of death is not the same as to sit in the shadow of death; one who sits in the shadow of death is firmly fixed in that shadow and strengthened in evil. On account of this, he is in darkness and lacks mercy so that the light may rise for him. He who does not sit, but who passes or walks through the midst of the shadow of death, not standing and hurrying across, does not walk alone because the Lord goes with him.[8]

As the old liturgical sentence says, "Jesus Christ is the light of the world, the light no darkness can overcome." May He continue to guide you, illuminating the darkness, as you go through life in His name. Amen.

---

[8] Ancient Christian Commentary on Scripture, vol. NT/VII, p. 179

05/15/2020 – *A Table Prepared* – *The Word* – Psalms 23:5

Psalms 23:5

> 5 You prepare a table before me in the presence of my enemies; you anoint my head with oil; my cup overflows. (ESV)

"Thou preparest a table before me in the presence of my enemies," David wrote. What a strange way of dealing with those things which seek to harm and destroy.

There is no doubt that Christianity has enemies. We know that the devil, the world, and our own sinful flesh conspire to pull us from the love of God. We have seen this with some of the orders given by states and cities concerning public worship during the present pandemic. Though various courts have struck down the orders which singled out Christians, the threat remains, and is a wake-up call.

Yet, God, rather than building a wall around His followers, does something extraordinary. He prepares a banquet. Martin Luther compares the banquet to the Word of God. He wrote:

> The more raging and raving and insane they are toward me, the less I worry about them; yes, instead, I am secure, happy, and cheerful. And that is true only because I have Thy Word. It gives me such strength and comfort in the presence of all my enemies, so that even when they rage and rave most violently, I feel more at ease than when I am sitting at a table and have all that my heart desires: food, drink, joy, pleasures, music, and the like.[9]

As we hold firmly to the Word of God, we are assured of our final victory through Christ Jesus, our Lord. Though our enemies may even take our life, we are assured of heaven because Jesus died and rose again to pay the price of our sins.

Is there a greater comfort than this banquet of God's Word? Amen.

---

[9] Luther's Works, American Edition: Vol. 12, p. 172

05/18/2020 – *A Table Prepared – The Sacrament* – Psalms 23:5

Psalms 23:5

> 5 You prepare a table before me in the presence of my enemies; you anoint my head with oil; my cup overflows. (ESV)

When David wrote, "Thou preparest a table before me in the presence of my enemies," he certainly had in mind the comfort which God brings His people in the midst of trouble. Under the Old Testament sacrificial system, the person offering the sacrifice received the benefit of the sacrifice by eating. We see this in the Passover recorded in Exodus.

As Christians, we rightly think of the Lord's Supper when we read of a banquet prepared by God. We are the invited guests, God serves us with the heavenly blessings earned by Jesus' death on the cross. He is the ultimate sacrifice, that to which the sacrifices of the Old Testament pointed.

As Lutherans, we believe, teach, and confess that the Lord's Supper is Christ's work, prepared for us to give the forgiveness of our sins. In the same way the Children of Israel ate the Passover lamb, so we are given the true body and blood of Jesus in and under the bread and wine. We therefore find comfort that, through this table prepared for us in the presence of our enemies, the devil, the world, and our own sinful flesh are defeated.

This banquet gives us tangible proof of God's rich grace, love, and mercy. This banquet gives us the forgiveness of sins, and thus the gift of life everlasting.

Amen.

05/20/2020 – *A Table Prepared* – *The Church* – Psalms 23:5

Psalms 23:5

> 5 You prepare a table before me in the presence of my enemies; you anoint my head with oil; my cup overflows. (ESV)

David, the shepherd-king, was a prophet. As he wrote, "You prepare a table before me in the presence of my enemies; you anoint my head with oil; my cup overflows," he wrote ultimately of the church.

We confess that the church is the people of God gathered around His Word and sacraments. Lutherans traditionally say there are two sacraments, actions commanded by Jesus which bring the forgiveness of sins, having visible elements. The two are baptism and the Lord's Supper, both of which have visible elements connected with the Word of God. This verse by David reminds us of both sacraments.

The table recalls the altar from which we are served the elements of the Lord's Supper. The anointing oil recalls our baptism when we were anointed with water and the name of the Triune God. In both sacraments, God's love, grace, and mercy overflow.

The Good Shepherd who provides green pasture and still waters gives to us the forgiveness of sins and life everlasting. His mercy endures forever, His love is a gift given for the sake of Christ Jesus. As His lambs, as the sheep of His pasture, we are protected from the evil of this world, and look to the promise of heaven.

May our Lord comfort you with these words of David. Amen.

05/22/2020 – *Dwelling in the House of the Lord* – Psalms 23:6

Psalms 23:6

> 6 Surely goodness and mercy shall follow me all the days of my life, and I shall dwell in the house of the LORD forever. (ESV)

If the Lord is indeed my shepherd, what is the final outcome? We know that He provides for our needs of body and soul, the green pastures and still waters. Our sins are forgiven for the sake of the death of Christ Jesus, which restores our souls.

Because we are part of God's flock, we do not fear that which may harm, but trust in God to protect us, to keep us ultimately safe from eternal death. He protects us from the devil, the world, and our own sinful flesh, though we certainly still give in to temptation.

Ultimately, then, we shall dwell with the Shepherd in His kingdom. We are assured of this because of God's grace, as shown by the redemption earned for us by Jesus.

Being the lamb of the Good Shepherd means we trust in Him above all things, knowing that our lives are in His loving hands. That is a comforting place to be. Amen.

05/25/2020 – *Lord, Teach Us to Pray* – Luke 11:1

Luke 11:1

> 1 Now Jesus was praying in a certain place, and when he finished, one of his disciples said to him, "Lord, teach us to pray, as John taught his disciples." (ESV)

During these dark and lonely days while visited by this pestilence, many people turn to God in prayer, asking that He relieve our suffering. This is good and right, for we believe we are indeed helpless before God, that we do not have the complete knowledge or power to save ourselves, either physically or spiritually.

What is prayer? Martin Luther wrote:

> All teachers of the Scriptures conclude that prayer is nothing else than the lifting up of heart or mind to God.[10]

Prayer is a response of faith, a response to God's grace and mercy. Because we believe that God loved us enough to send His Son to bear the price of our sin, we believe and trust that He will hear our cries.

Thus all prayers are first and foremost offered in the name of Jesus, or in the clear understanding that we are reconciled to our heavenly Father through Him. If we pray thinking we will be heard because of our own righteousness, we will be sadly mistaken.

Over the next few weeks we will be looking at prayer in general, and the Lord's Prayer in particular. Even as we pray that God grants wisdom to our leaders, healing to this land, and strength to meet the problems of this day, we do so confident of God's love towards us.

May our heavenly Father grant you the peace of knowing that He is the source of all our blessings. Amen.

---

[10] Luther's Works, American Edition, Vol. 42, page 25

05/27/2020 – *Rejoice Always* – 1 Thessalonians 5:16–18

1 Thessalonians 5:16–18

> 16 Rejoice always,
>
> 17 pray without ceasing,
>
> 18 give thanks in all circumstances; for this is the will of God in Christ Jesus for you. (ESV)

The Bible has a lot to say about prayer. Saint Paul, in his first epistle to the church in Thessalonica, wrote: "Rejoice always, pray without ceasing, give thanks in all circumstances; for this is the will of God in Christ Jesus for you."

This sounds like another time where we are given instructions impossible to follow. During this pestilence, how are we supposed to rejoice always? Daily we receive the news of disease and death and we watch the numbers climb. Will this nation turn into a vast wasteland, filled with ghost towns as hoards drop in the street? That seems to be the message of the media.

Suffering is a gift from God which calls us back to Him, which shows us the truth of original sin. The daily news reports tell us of the wages of sin; that, in the end we all suffer temporal death.

But we rejoice for Christ Jesus has overcome temporal death on our behalf. He has opened the way of everlasting life because He earned for us salvation through His suffering and death. The destruction we see today is temporal, the blessings of God are eternal.

Therefore, we can rejoice, knowing of God's rich grace, love, and mercy. In spite of present appearances, we know that our Lord has granted us the forgiveness of sins as a gift. Where there is forgiveness, there is life.

May our Lord grant you His rich grace and comfort, that you may know and trust in Him. Amen.

05/29/2020 – *Now Thank We All Our God* – 1 Thessalonians 5:16–18

1 Thessalonians 5:16–18

> 16 Rejoice always,
>
> 17 pray without ceasing,
>
> 18 give thanks in all circumstances; for this is the will of God in Christ Jesus for you. (ESV)

The Thanksgiving hymn, *Now Thank We All Our God,* was written by Martin Rinckart during the Thirty Years War, which lasted from 1618 through 1648. During the war, in 1637, the city of Eilenberg, where Rinckart was a pastor, was also struck by the plague.

At the height of the plague, over 8,000 people died, including Rinckart's wife. Rinckart, the only surviving pastor in the city, performed over 4,000 funerals, often for up to fifty people during a single day.

Yet Rinckart saw the hope of the resurrection, that through Jesus' death comes life everlasting. This hymn, which was first a meal prayer written for his children, clearly proclaims what God has done to bless and keep us.

In the midst of tragedy and death, Rinckart saw life.[11] God's blessings are eternal, after the night dawns a new and glorious day. Thus we are bold to say with Saint Paul, "Rejoice always, pray without ceasing, give thanks in all circumstances; for this is the will of God in Christ Jesus for you."

Amen.

---

[11] Drawn from *The LSB Hymnal Companion,* vol. 1, p. 1418.

6/016/2020 – *Pray Without Ceasing* – 1 Thessalonians 5:16–18

1 Thessalonians 5:16–18

16 Rejoice always,

17 pray without ceasing,

18 give thanks in all circumstances; for this is the will of God in Christ Jesus for you. (ESV)

When Saint Paul wrote, "pray without ceasing," he certainly did not mean that we needed to be on our knees twenty-four hours a day. Indeed, Paul made tents, which was hard, physical labor, requiring that he concentrate on the work at hand.

However, prayer is the fruit of a believer's faith in the gracious forgiveness of sins for Christ's sake. It is continuous because the heart is led and moved by the Holy Spirit, continually turned toward God.

A Christian prays even when not aware of that prayer, as when working. A Christian prays even in times of trouble when he thinks himself incapable of prayer. A Christian prays even as he works all to the glory of God, realizing that even the most humble of tasks, done with the thought that it serves our neighbors, is a prayer of thanksgiving and praise.

In this way, as we fulfill our daily lives, we are in constant prayer. Even more-so, we set aside times each day to lift up our hearts to God, to pray, praise, and give thanks in His name.

May you be continually blessed as your life is, in both word and deed, a life of prayer. Amen.

06/03/2020 – *God Hears Our Prayers* – 1 Thessalonians 5:16–18

1 Thessalonians 5:16–18

> 16 Rejoice always,
>
> 17 pray without ceasing,
>
> 18 give thanks in all circumstances; for this is the will of God in Christ Jesus for you. (ESV)

There are two types of Christian prayer, prayers of supplication and prayers of thanksgiving. While we can break prayers into more categories, these two work well as a framework.

We are told to pray for our leaders and for the good of all people. We are told to pray for fellow believers, and for those who have not yet come to faith in Christ Jesus. We are told to pray for physical blessings, our daily bread, so to speak, and the spiritual blessings of forgiveness, wisdom, and faith.

Only those who know the comfort of God's gracious love through Jesus Christ can come before Him in prayer. Our advocate with the Father is His Son, who died and rose again for our salvation. All other prayers, the superstitions which arise from experience with certain objects or incantations, are not heard.

As we pray for spiritual blessings, we pray with confidence that our prayers are in accordance with God's holy and loving will. As we pray for physical blessings, we do so knowing that our desires may not be in our own best interests. Thus we pray, "Thy will be done."

God hears our prayer, even when He, in His infinite wisdom, declares the answer to be "no." At all times, our prayers are answered in a way that brings the highest good.

We pray without ceasing, confident that our loving Father seeks to do that which brings us the ultimate blessing. Amen.

06/05/2020 – *Give Thanks* – 1 Thessalonians 5:16–18

1 Thessalonians 5:16–18

16 Rejoice always,

17 pray without ceasing,

18 give thanks in all circumstances; for this is the will of God in Christ Jesus for you. (ESV)

As we divide prayers into two groups, supplication and thanksgiving, we know that it is a good thing to give thanks unto the Lord, our God.

Sometimes thanking God is difficult. We are bound up in the moment; we see disease, destruction, and isolation. Yet, our Lord uses even these distressing times to call us back to Himself. We are reminded, time and again, that we are not in control, that we cannot rely only on ourselves.

Even the most horrible of circumstances, the miscarriage of justice which caused an innocent, sinless Man to be crucified, to suffer, and to die, brings the ultimate good. Where the devil, the world, and our own flesh rejoiced to see Jesus silenced and hidden away in the tomb, this was His ultimate victory on our behalf. What the disciples feared was the end on Good Friday was shown the beginning of life on Easter.

Thus we thank the Lord, even in the midst of trouble, for He is good. We hear Paul's words, "give thanks in all circumstances," and know that our sins are forgiven for Christ' sake. We know that our suffering is temporary, and we will live eternally in God's heavenly mansions. Amen.

06/08/2020 – *Our Father – Part 1* – Matthew 6:9

Matthew 6:9

> 9 Pray then like this: Our Father in heaven, hallowed be your name. (ESV)

How do we pray? The disciples of Jesus asked Him this question. We continue to ask that question, even 2000 years after the resurrection of Jesus. It is a fundamental right and duty of Christians to pray, but we are often confused as to what this means.

Jesus, Himself, gave us the framework and words of prayer, recorded both by Matthew and Luke.

> Pray then like this: Our Father in heaven, hallowed be your name.[12]
> Matthew 6:9

How is it possible that we can call upon God as our Father? Is He not the creator of heaven and earth? Is He not all powerful, all knowing, almighty, and holy? Yet Saint Paul reminded the church in Galatia, "for in Christ Jesus you are all sons of God, through faith."[13] Galatians 3:26

Also Saint John wrote:

> See what kind of love the Father has given to us, that we should be called children of God; and so we are. The reason why the world does not know us is that it did not know him.[14] 1 John 3:1

Therefore, we are bold to pray to our heavenly Father, both because we have been redeemed by Christ Jesus, and because we have been adopted by our Father through the working of the Holy Spirit. It is our privilege to approach the throne of the Almighty and speak to Him as we would to our loving Father.

Such is the privilege of a Christian. Amen.

---

[12] Matthew 6:9 (ESV)
[13] Galatians 3:26 (ESV)
[14] I John 3:1 (ESV)

06/10/2020 – *Our Father – Part 2* – Matthew 6:9

Matthew 6:9

9 Pray then like this: Our Father in heaven, hallowed be your name. (ESV)

So Christians pray to our heavenly Father, as Jesus told us to do. Our heavenly Father is the perfect father, ready to hear, always loving, truly present. Unlike earthly fathers, who fail at fatherhood because they are sinful and unclean, our heavenly Father truly loves and cares for us at all times.

Yet, there are times when our heavenly Father seems to ignore our prayers. We don't seem to get what we want, that which overwhelms us is not removed. Does that mean that God actually is too busy?

No. Our prayers for temporal blessings may prove harmful in the long run. As a loving Father, first and foremost in His will is our eternal blessings and good. Sometimes a father has to say "no" to keep his loving children from harm and danger. Sometimes a father has to allow his children to suffer defeat and pain so that they are strengthened, so that they may know that which is harmful.

One of the hymns for the season of Lent[15]ays:

```
    When we seem in vain to pray
  And our hope seems far away,
  In the darkness be our stay.
  Hear us, Holy Jesus.
    LSB 447 – Jesus, in Your Dying Woes: vs 11
```

Our heavenly Father hears our prayers and answers each one, knowing that His answer is always for the ultimate good for His beloved children.

May God continue to grant you faith that you may approach Him as children approach their loving father. Amen.

---

[15] s

06/13/2020 – *Our Father – Part 3* – Matthew 6:9

Matthew 6:9

> 9 Pray then like this: Our Father in heaven, hallowed be your name. (ESV)

If Jesus said, "Pray then like this: Our Father in heaven, hallowed be your name," what of the prayers we seem to utter to others? Are such prayers effective?

Let's go back to the First Commandment, "You shall have no other gods before me."[16] Exodus 20:3 We believe, teach, and confess that there is no other God than the Triune God, Father, Son, and Holy Spirit. To hold firmly in faith to the Triune God is to trust fully, completely, and only in Him. Because our heavenly Father is intimately interested in His dear children, we have no need to pray to anyone else.

Our Lutheran *Small Catechism* puts it simply, "We pray only to the one true God, Father, Son, and Holy Spirit (and not to idols, ancestors, saints, angels, or anything else God has created)."[17] This may go against the practice and teachings of others, but nowhere are we directed to pray elsewhere. Jesus invites us to pray to our Father in heaven, and because of the Triune nature of God, one God but three Persons, to each Person of the Trinity, individually or collectively.

Thus we are bold to pray, "Our Father," knowing that He loves us and hears us and answers us. May our Lord grant you faith to call upon Him in all troubles, to pray for others, to pray for yourself, to confess your sins, and to praise Him for His goodness. Amen.

---

[16] Exodus 20:3 (ESV)
[17] Luther, M. (2018). *Luther's Small Catechism with explanation.* St. Louis, CPH: p. 239

06/15/2020 – *Our Father – Part 4* – Matthew 6:9

Matthew 6:9

> 9 Pray then like this: Our Father in heaven, hallowed be your name. (ESV)

Individual Christians pray to their heavenly Father for temporal and spiritual blessings. Frequently and properly the praying Christian says "I," speaking of personal needs and desires. This is good, right, and salutary so to do.

Why, then, does Jesus invite us to pray to "Our Father?" There are at least two reasons, both of which bring comfort and joy, both of which increase our trust that God hears and answers our prayers.

Saint John reminds us:

> My little children, I am writing these things to you so that you may not sin. But if anyone does sin, we have an advocate with the Father, Jesus Christ the righteous.[18] 1 John 2:1

When we pray "Our Father," we join with our adopted brother, our advocate, Jesus Christ. Our prayers are in concert with Him; we never pray alone. Prayers are heard though Jesus Christ, and we approach our heavenly Father with Him by our side, encouraging, helping, and praying with us.

As Christians, we are part of the family of all believers. Though we bring personal petitions to God, we always pray for all who are saved by God's rich grace through faith for the sake of Christ. We say "Our" because we are not alone, but represent each of our brothers and sisters in faith.

Can there be any greater comfort, knowing that Jesus prays with us, and that each of our family in Christ is praying for us? Thus we boldly pray, "Our Father." Amen.

---

[18] I John 2:1 (ESV)

06/17/2020 – *Our Father* – Part 5 – Matthew 6:9

Matthew 6:9

> 9 Pray then like this: Our Father in heaven, hallowed be your name. (ESV)

Jesus said, "Pray then like this: Our Father in heaven, hallowed be your name." Is this the only way to pray, the only words we can use? Certainly not.

King David wrote, 1400 years before the birth of Jesus, "and call upon me in the day of trouble; I will deliver you, and you shall glorify me."[19] Psalms 50:15 When we are in trouble, we don't take the time to fall on our knees, to use memorized words, to adopt a formal style of prayer. When we are in trouble we may simply cry out, "God help me." That prayer is heard.

An old hymn[20] reminds us:

```
    With the Lord begin Your task;
Jesus will direct it.
For His aid and counsel ask;
Jesus will perfect it.
Every morn with Jesus rise,
And when day is ended,
In His name then close your eyes;
be to Him commended.
    LSB 869 – With the Lord Begin Your Task: vs. 1
```

We therefore pray to our heavenly Father, through and with our Savior, knowing that He will hear our prayers, that He will answer in the way that is best for us and for all believers. No matter the words we use, we pray, trusting our heavenly Father, knowing that He is loving and gracious. Amen.

---

[19] Psalms 50:15 (ESV)
[20] r

06/19/2020 – *Hallowed Be Thy Name – Part 1* – Matthew 6:9

Matthew 6:9

> 9 Pray then like this: Our Father in heaven, hallowed be your name. (ESV)

Jesus said, "Pray then like this: Our Father in heaven, hallowed be your name." As Christians, our concern is to ensure that God's name is kept holy among us, that it is held with honor in all the world.

How is God's name kept holy? Should we, like some, never utter the name of God so that we do not misuse His name? After all, doesn't the Commandment say, "Thou shalt not take the name of the Lord thy God in vain?" By never using God's name, we think we are keeping the Commandment, we are seeing the first petition of the Lord's Prayer being fulfilled.

But the name of God is more than a simple word. God has more than one name, as Isaiah wrote:

> For to us a child is born, to us a son is given; and the government shall be upon his shoulder, and his name shall be called Wonderful Counselor, Mighty God, Everlasting Father, Prince of Peace.[21] Isaiah 9:6

God's name is anything which reveals Him to the world. Thus we pray that His name be holy among us, used properly, and be held in reverence.

May our Lord bless your desire to properly use His name, which reflects the gift of faith given to you for the sake of Christ Jesus. Amen.

---

[21] Isaiah 9:6 (ESV)

06/22/2020 – *Hallowed Be Thy Name – Part 2* – Matthew 6:9

Matthew 6:9

9 Pray then like this: Our Father in heaven, hallowed be your name. (ESV)

Jesus said, "Pray then like this: Our Father in heaven, hallowed be your name."

How do we misuse God's name, how is it profaned among us? There are a number of ways, done both in word and actions. In the first place, God's name is profaned when it is used to teach lies, falsehoods, or to cause confusion. There are cases throughout history of pastors and popular preachers who take Bible passages out of context to promote a non-Christian teaching.

Consider the pastor who says, "This passage does not apply because it is poetry, and poetry does not teach us doctrine." Where do we find that standard? Didn't Jesus quote the Psalms, did He not quote poetry, to tell us that He is the Son of God? Didn't He say, "The stone that the builders rejected has become the cornerstone?" That is from Psalm 118, and it tells us that Jesus, who was rejected by the religious leaders of the day, is the cornerstone of His Church.

The flippant, "Oh my God," or the shorthand "OMG" trivializes the holy name of God. That which is precious is not used without thinking.

God's name is profaned when we act against His holy will, when we live in a way that does not bring credit to Him. We are adopted by God through baptism, thus all we do reflects on Him.

So we pray, "hallowed be Thy name" both that God's rich grace may be in this world, and that we might properly honor that which reveals Him to us. Amen.

06/24/2020 – *Hallowed Be Thy Name* – Part 3 – Matthew 6:9

Matthew 6:9

9 Pray then like this: Our Father in heaven, hallowed be your name. (ESV)

If we pray, "hallowed by Thy name," and we believe, teach, and confess that we can use God's name, how is this done? God's name is holy among us through both word and action.

As Christians, we speak the truth about God's Word. We confess that the Bible is His inspired Word, that it is true. When we disagree with the Bible, we realize that it is our own sinful nature rebelling against God, thus we repent. "Did God really say" is answered as we daily study His Word, as we diligently read, mark, study, and learn so to better understand His Word.

Knowing God's holy Word, knowing about His name is meaningless if we do not strive to live according to His good and gracious will. God's name is held holy among us as we seek to serve Him by reflecting His love toward our neighbors.

If God's name is important to us, if His Word is held in high esteem, we will naturally desire to live for Him. This desire to live in accordance with God's desires is one of the gifts of God, given to us by His great love alone.

May God richly bless you with His favor as we keep His name holy in both word and deed. Amen.

06/26/2020 – *Thy Kingdom Come* – Part 1 – Matthew 6:10

Matthew 6:10

10 Your kingdom come, your will be done, on earth as it is in heaven. (ESV)

As Jesus taught His disciples to pray, He told them to ask, "Thy kingdom come." Seeing the first petitions of the Lord's Prayer echo the first tablet of the Ten Commandments, we must ask, "what is the kingdom of God?" For what are we praying?

One of the clearest answers to this question comes from Martin Luther in his *Large Catechism:*

> But what is God's kingdom? Answer, "Nothing other than what we learned in the Creed: God sent His Son, Jesus Christ, our Lord, into the world to redeem us from the devil's power. He sent Him to bring us to Himself and to govern us as a King of righteousness, life, and salvation against sin, death, and an evil conscience."[22]

What better prayer can we utter that we may live for Christ and receive all the blessings which He gives; forgiveness of sins and life everlasting? Amen.

---

[22] *Book of Concord – Reader's Edition*, CPH, p. 440

06/29/2020 – *Thy Kingdom Come* – Part 2 – Matthew 6:10

Matthew 6:10

10 Your kingdom come, your will be done, on earth as it is in heaven. (ESV)

The kingdom of God is not a New Testament idea, some change in the way that God relates to His people. We find the promise of an everlasting kingdom throughout the Old Testament.

In Exodus we read the confession of the Children of Israel that God would reign forever. King David received the promise that one of his descendants would be on the throne forever, as also Isaiah prophesied. Time and again the Old Testament prophets spoke of Jesus as the everlasting King.

The kingdom of God was ushered in to history when Jesus was born of the virgin Mary, lived, died, and rose again. Being true God and true man, of the lineage of David, Jesus fulfilled the words and promises of the Old Testament.

Today the kingdom of God comes to us through the Word and Sacraments. Jesus promised, as recorded in the last verses of Matthew, "I will be with you always, even unto the end of the age."

Therefore, as we pray, "Thy kingdom come," we pray for the success of the message of God's grace and love, that all people may come to believe in Him, trusting Christ Jesus as their Redeemer. Amen.

07/01/2020 – *Thy Will Be Done – Part 1* – Matthew 6:10

Matthew 6:10

10 Your kingdom come, your will be done, on earth as it is in heaven. (ESV)

When we pray, "Thy will be done," we first must determine if we can know God's will. What does God want? Can we resist God's will?

God is irresistible when He works directly within this world. Creation was done at His command. The final judgment will indeed have no appeal. When God demands, there is no resistance.

However, God has chosen to work through means and not by direct revelation. He comes to us in Word and Sacrament, using the voice of the pastor to proclaim His grace and mercy. Faith is created through the Word and water of baptism, and strengthened with the Word connected to the bread and wine of the Lord's Supper.

Although God would have all people be saved and come to the knowledge of the truth[23] 1 Timothy 2:4 because He works through the Church, we can resist His will. This simple fact assures us that salvation is through Christ alone, that those who are condemned are condemned by their own will and unbelief.

Thus, in this petition of the Lord's prayer we ask that our will conform to His, that His name be holy among us, and that His kingdom reign within us. God grant that His good and gracious will be done. Amen.

---

[23] 1 Timothy 2:4

07/03/2020 – *Thy Will Be Done – Part 2* – Matthew 6:10

Matthew 6:10

10 Your kingdom come, your will be done, on earth as it is in heaven. (ESV)

We are in a constant state of warfare between the world, the devil, and our own sinful flesh. Even Christians desire to be in charge, to demand that God conform Himself to our will rather than we conform to His.

When you consider that the devil, the world, and our own flesh seek the best for themselves rather than the good of others, we can see that our will leads to conflict and death. God, however, desires that all good be done for those who have not rejected Him. His will is that everything, be it good or evil, eventually work for the benefit of those who have faith in Jesus Christ.

So God created a world which He called "good," but man defaced this creation. God created mankind in His image, holy and perfect, but man wanted more and rebelled. God created light, but we want the darkness to hide our inmost shame.

When we pray, "Thy will be done," we ask God to grant that all things work for our eternal benefit. Even the pains, sorrows, and persecution of this life prepare us for the blessings of life everlasting for the sake of Jesus.

When we pray, "Thy will be done," we acknowledge that the greatest evil, the death of the Son of God, gave the greatest good, the salvation of all sinners.

May God's will be done in our lives, in this world, and for all eternity. Amen.

07/06/2020 – *Thy Will Be Done – Part 3* – Matthew 6:10

Matthew 6:10

10 Your kingdom come, your will be done, on earth as it is in heaven. (ESV)

If we pray, "Thy will be done," does this mean that God causes the problems of this world? Can we lay the pandemic at His feet, along with the racial tension and social unrest that have so gripped this nation? If God's will is for the good, why the evil which we see?

We are at war between God and sin. The devil, the world, and our own sinful flesh seek to destroy everything God has done, and seek to go against His will.

Did not Jesus die for all people regardless of race? Did His suffering and death not pay the price of their sin? God equally loves everyone, loves each individual, enough to sacrifice His Son for their good. In our sin, however, we claim superiority over people based on the accident of ethnic background or other meaningless criteria.

In protest, those who seek respect sinfully destroy that which God has made. As we pray, "Thy will be done," we certainly pray that we respect each person and love them and build them up as Christ loves us. It is God's good and gracious will that we love our neighbor as ourselves, seeking good for all people even at personal cost.

May we reflect God's good and gracious will as we deal with each other, as we serve Him by serving our neighbors. Amen.

07/08/2020 – *Give Us This Day Our Daily Bread – Part 1* – Matthew 6:11

Matthew 6:11

11 Give us this day our daily bread, (ESV)

We have determined that God's good and gracious will extends not only for our spiritual and eternal benefit, but also to this life. Therefore Jesus taught His disciples to pray, "Give us this day our daily bread."

Martin Luther wrote:

> God provides daily bread, even to the wicked, without our prayer, but we pray in this petition that God may make us aware of His gifts and enable us to receive our daily bread with thanksgiving.[24]

Our heavenly Father, who sent His Son to redeem us from sin and eternal death, certainly will care for His creation. Here, again, God works through means. Every helping profession, be it in agriculture to produce our food, or transportation to deliver our food, or sales to stockpile and deliver all we need, is honorable. Every lawful profession serves God by serving each other.

Therefore, even though we earn our daily bread through our labors, it ultimately comes from God as His gracious gift. We thank and praise Him for all His benefits. Amen.

---

[24] Small Catechism, Fourth Petition – Tappert

07/10/2020 – *Give Us This Day Our Daily Bread – Part 2* – Matthew 6:11

Matthew 6:11

11 Give us this day our daily bread, (ESV)

Martin Luther wrote:

> When you pray this petition ["give us this day our daily bread"] turn your eyes to everything that can prevent our bread from coming and the crops from prospering. Therefore extend your thoughts to all the fields and do not see only the baker's oven. You pray, therefore, against the devil and the world, who can hinder the grain by tempest and war. We pray also for temporal peace against war, because in times of war we cannot have bread. Likewise, you pray for government, for sustenance and peace, without which you cannot eat: Grant, Lord, that the grain may prosper, that the princes may keep the peace, that war may not break out, that we may give thanks to thee in peace. Therefore it would be proper to stamp the emperor's or the princes' coat-of-arms upon bread as well as upon money or coins.[25]

Can there be a better prayer than this? Amen.

---

[25] Martin Luther, Sermon on the Lord's Prayer (1528). LW 51:176-177

07/13/2020 – *Give Us This Day Our Daily Bread – Part 3* – Matthew 6:11

Matthew 6:11

11 Give us this day our daily bread, (ESV)

In these days of political divide, this prayer, "Give us this day our daily bread," becomes even more important. With this prayer we not only ask for good food and clean water, but also we pray for those who govern us, who make and judge our laws. We pray for peace in this land, that may have the best for all people.

Because we believe, teach, and confess that God has placed people in charge for our own good, even if we disagree with them, we treat the office and person with respect and honor. Without good and wise leaders, from the local authorities such as the mayor, city council, and school board, to the president of these United States, our lives would not be blessed.

Therefore, this petition includes the prayer that our Lord richly bless our leaders with wisdom to know that which is right, and the courage to act on our behalf even if it is a difficult path. We also pray that we trust them and hold them in proper esteem. Our leaders are under great pressure to act in ways contrary to wisdom, thus they need our prayers at all times.

In this country, our prayer includes that we act as good citizens, voting when given the opportunity, interacting with those we have elected, and being informed on the various questions of the day. In this way we serve our neighbors and ensure they also receive their daily bread. Amen.

07/15/2020 – *Forgive Us Our Trespasses* – Part 1 – Matthew 6:12

Matthew 6:12

12 and forgive us our debts, as we also have forgiven our debtors. (ESV)

When using the Lord's Prayer in a setting where people of different denominations are gathered, it is a good thing to print the words which are used. Because the Lord's Prayer was recorded both in Matthew and Luke, there are some variations in the way we have learned it. Some people pray, "forgive us our trespasses," while others intone, "forgive us our debts." Both are correct translations of the prayer as recorded by Matthew. Luke, on the other hand, says, "forgive us our sins," using a different word in the Greek, but meaning exactly the same thing as Matthew's text.

Certainly, Jesus would have spoken of this prayer multiple times when He taught His disciples. The context of the giving of the prayer in Matthew and Luke are different, thus both authors are accurately recording our Lord's words.

The truth is, we have indeed sinned against God and neighbor in thought, word, and deed. We cannot pay the price of our sin, but ask God, in His grace and mercy, to forgive our sins for the sake of the suffering, death, and resurrection of Jesus Christ. It is only because of God's great love that we are forgiven, declared holy and perfect in God's sight. This is the peace which passes all understanding, that God, in His mercy, had given to you eternal life.

God grant you this peace now and forever. Amen.

07/17/2020 – *Forgive Us Our Trespasses – Part 2* – Matthew 6:12

Matthew 6:12

12 and forgive us our debts, as we also have forgiven our debtors. (ESV)

We pray, "forgive us our trespasses," or "forgive us our debts," knowing that God will answer with a resounding "yes." Because His good and gracious will is for all people to be saved and come to the knowledge of the truth, because His good and gracious will is for His kingdom to come now and for eternity, we are assured of our salvation from sin and death.

No sin is so horrible that it cannot be forgiven for the sake of the suffering and death of Jesus. Even while He was being nailed to the cross, Jesus prayed that the people executing the sinless Son of God be forgiven of their sin, that even the sin of murdering the incarnate Son of God was not unforgivable.

When Jesus pronounced absolution, the forgiveness of sins, it was unconditional. The criminal who came to faith while hanging on the cross next to Jesus was completely pardoned. The various women accused of adultery were absolved, their sin remembered no more. Even Judas could have been forgiven in the same way Peter was forgiven, but Judas rejected God's gift of grace.

Where there is forgiveness, where your sins, all of your sins, are not counted against you, you will find life everlasting. This is the promise of the Gospel, the hope of all who trust in Christ Jesus as their Redeemer. Amen.

07/20/2020 – *Forgive Us Our Trespasses – Part 3* – Matthew 6:12

Matthew 6:12

12 and forgive us our debts, as we also have forgiven our debtors. (ESV)

In our prayer, "forgive us our trespasses," we add "as we forgive those who trespass against us." This does not make forgiveness conditional on our actions. Rather, we are asking God to treat us in the way we treat others. We are asking God to give us the strength to forgive as we are forgiven, completely and utterly, without reservation.

Because we live in a sinful world, because we selfishly act against God and neighbor, we constantly need the assurance that we are forgiven. Because others sin against us, we reflect God's love to them.

Some use the term, "pay it forward," to describe passing the good we receive to those in need. This is a great illustration. We have been forgiven, therefore we "pay it forward" to those who sin against us. We also forgive because we know that all things in this life are temporary, that our true hope is eternal, not tied to this earth. Therefore we can forgive as forgiven, for our eyes are on Christ Jesus, not on our own selfish desires.

This prayer, "forgive us our trespasses as we forgive those who trespass against us," provides a framework to show respect to both God and neighbor. Even when we are sinned against, the person causing offense is also loved by God, thus we seek their good rather than harm. This helps us to put all things into perspective, that we are the hands of God spreading His love in this sin-sickened world.

May God give you the strength to forgive as forgiven, to reflect His grace at all times for the sake of Jesus Christ. Amen.

07/22/2020 – *Forgive Us Our Trespasses* – Part 5 – Matthew 6:12

Matthew 6:12

12 and forgive us our debts, as we also have forgiven our debtors. (ESV)

Our prayer, "forgive us our trespasses," is an expression of our belief that God has given us salvation, a gift we did not earn. We do not present our goodness to God, for we confess that we have no goodness apart from Him. Therefore this prayer speaks of our faith that the death of Jesus Christ is sufficient to cover our sins against God and man.

Throughout the Bible we see God's love, His grace, His forgiveness given to those who acknowledge their sin and turn to Him. For sinners in the Old Testament, such as King David, forgiveness was given in light of the coming Christ Jesus. For sinners in the New Testament forgiveness is given because Jesus indeed died and rose again as an accomplished fact.

Because we are forgiven, we forgive. In the same way that God does not hold our sins against us, we pray for the strength to fully forgive when someone has offended us. We do not retaliate, we do not hold grudges, we forgive completely.

May our Lord give you the ability to forgive as you are forgiven, that you may live in peace with your friends, family, and neighbors. Amen.

07/24/2020 – *Lead Us Not Into Temptation – Part 1* – Matthew 6:13

Matthew 6:13

13 And lead us not into temptation, but deliver us from evil. (ESV)

As we speak the Lord's Prayer, we come upon a petition which seems, on the surface, to be contrary to what we learned about God. "Lead us not into temptation" suggests that God tempts us to sin, that God gives us the opportunity to sin. This certainly is not true, for God desires that we be holy, that we turn from sin and cling only to Him.

This is one of the cases where the English translation is not as clear as the original Greek. We could translate this phrase as "do not let us be brought into temptation," a request that we be guarded from all assaults by the devil, the world, and our own sinful flesh.

Martin Luther wrote:

> God, indeed, tempts no one; but we pray in this petition that God would guard and keep us, so that the devil, the world, and our flesh may not deceive us, nor seduce us into misbelief, despair, and other great shame and vice; and though we be assailed by them, that still we may finally overcome and gain the victory.[26]

Thus we ask the God who saved us because of His great love, would, for the sake of Jesus Christ, strengthen and preserve us as we trust in Him and serve our neighbors. May our Lord continue to be with you, that you may stand firm against the temptations which daily attempt to draw us from Him. Amen.

---

[26]http://bookofconcord.org/smallcatechismhp#lordsprayer

07/27/2020 – *Lead Us Not Into Temptation – Part 2* – Matthew 6:13

Matthew 6:13

13 And lead us not into temptation, but deliver us from evil. (ESV)

We have determined that God does not tempt anyone. Temptations come from three sources, the devil, the world, and our own sinful flesh. All three are in opposition to God, all three seek to overthrow God and to be in charge.

When we pray, "lead us not into temptation," we are asking for God to bless us with the power and strength to resist. Even though we cannot escape temptation and tribulation, we pray that we may not give in to them or be overwhelmed by them.

Temptation comes from Satan, the devil, in the realm of conscience and spiritual matters. It was Satan who tempted Adam and Eve with the promise they would be like God. His purpose is to tear us from God's grace and mercy, to draw us into unbelief, false security, and stubbornness.

Because these assaults can be very subtle, we are always on guard to preserve our faith. How do we prepare for this daily temptation? The best way is to be in the Word of God, to daily study the Bible, to read again of God's grace and mercy. Add to that the practice of praying multiple times each day. We say back to God what He has said to us. In so doing, we reinforce our understanding of the truth of God's rich love.

May our Lord preserve you from the temptations of the devil, that you remain steadfast in the one true faith in Christ Jesus. Amen.

07/29/2020 – *Lead Us Not Into Temptation – Part 3* – Matthew 6:13

Matthew 6:13

13 And lead us not into temptation, but deliver us from evil. (ESV)

"Lead us not into temptation," we pray. Our adversaries are the devil, the world, and our own sinful flesh. Thus we ask God to protect us from temptation, to give us the power to recognize and overcome temptation.

The world was twisted by sin the day that Adam and Eve rebelled against God. Death, disease, and destruction corrupted creation. That which God saw as good was damaged.

Each day, the world attacks us through word and deed. It drives us to anger and impatience, a sort of spiritual road-rage. As Martin Luther wrote:

> In short, there is nothing but hatred and envy, enmity, violence and wrong, unfaithfulness, vengeance, cursing, raillery, slander, pride and haughtiness, with superfluous finery, honor, fame, and power, where no one is willing to be the least, but every one desires to sit at the head and to be seen before all.[27]

Though Luther wrote those words 490 years ago, they are as fresh as last night's news. Nothing has changed.

Jesus Christ brings peace into this sinful world, the peace of knowing our sins are forgiven for the sake of His bitter suffering and death. Because He has overcome death for us, we can face that which the world uses to tempt us to great despair.

May our Lord grant you strength in these days, to look first to Him, and to receive the peace of God in the face of temptation. Amen.

---

[27] Large Catechism, Sixth Petition

07/31/2020 – *Lead Us Not Into Temptation* – Part 4 – Matthew 6:13

Matthew 6:13

13 And lead us not into temptation, but deliver us from evil. (ESV)

Jesus taught us to pray, "Lead us not into temptation." Our enemies who would tear us from God's grace, love, and mercy are both spiritual and physical. The devil seeks our eternal condemnation. The world seeks our emotional downfall. Even our own sinful desires seek our destruction.

How often do we make resolutions to improve our lives, to take better care of our bodies? We promise to exercise so to forestall a heart attack or other grave illness. We promise to go on a diet to lose those extra pounds. We promise to get enough sleep, or to give up smoking, or to cut back on alcohol. The intentions of January first are forgotten by February, if not long before.

Martin Luther explained it this way:

> For in the flesh we dwell and carry the old Adam about our neck, who exerts himself and incites us daily to inchastity, laziness, gluttony and drunkenness, avarice and deception, to defraud our neighbor and to overcharge him, and, in short, to all manner of evil lusts which cleave to us by nature, and to which we are incited by the society, example and what we hear and see of other people, which often wound and inflame even an innocent heart.[28]

These temptations are with us all the time, we can't escape them. But being tempted is not harmful, giving in to temptation is sin. Accordingly, we must be armed and ready to confront all temptations, all desire to sin, both for our own good and for the good of those around us.

Thus we pray that we have the strength to overcome the temptations of the flesh. Amen.

---

[28] Large Catechism, Sixth Petition

08/03/2020 – *Lead Us Not Into Temptation* – *Part 5* – Matthew 6:13

Matthew 6:13

13 And lead us not into temptation, but deliver us from evil. (ESV)

Jesus taught us to pray, "Lead us not into temptation." As we have seen, temptations come from the devil, the world, and our own sinful flesh.

These temptations are with us all the time. We can't escape them. But being tempted is not harmful, giving in to temptation is sin. Accordingly, we must be armed and ready to confront all temptations, all desire to sin, both for our own good and for the good of those around us.

What do we do in the face of temptation? We pray, "Heavenly Father, you commanded me to pray; let me not fall because of temptation, for the sake of Your Son, Jesus Christ." Such prayers are pleasing in God's sight.

We arm ourselves with the sure and certain Word of God, pondering His grace and mercy. We shun that which is evil, seeking the good. Most of all, we hold firmly to God's promise of life everlasting, for Jesus Christ has overcome the devil, the world, and our own sinful flesh.

To God alone be the glory. Amen.

08/05/2020 – *But Deliver Us From Evil – Part 1* – Matthew 6:13

Matthew 6:13

13 And lead us not into temptation, but deliver us from evil. (ESV)

Scholars have long known that it is difficult, if not impossible, to translate works from one language to another. We can get close, but the subtle nuances are lost, and cultural references become very obscure. Even the working language of professionals sounds foreign to those outside the profession.

Yet we can certainly come up with an approximate translation, and get the sense of meaning for most of a book written in another language. Some words, however, will be completely lost, some concepts completely missing.

So we come to the phrase in the Lord's Prayer, "deliver us from evil." That seems straight forward, for we desire that no bad thing happens, but that we receive God's rich blessings. In this case, evil may be seen as a mindless thing, the changes and chances of this world.

But the Greek can be translated, "deliver us from the evil one." Now there is an intelligent being bent on our destruction, the one who first tempted Adam and Eve. There is a face and an intention for evil, an active enemy of all that is good and pure.

Which translation is better? Both are good, both speak of the ongoing spiritual battle between the faithful of God and the devil, the world, and our own sinful flesh.

May our Lord protect you from the changes and chances of this world, and the intentional evil of those who seek your destruction. Amen.

08/07/2020 – *But Deliver Us From Evil – Part 2* – Matthew 6:13

Matthew 6:13

13 And lead us not into temptation, but deliver us from evil. (ESV)

Jesus taught His disciples to pray, "but deliver us from evil." Is it appropriate to translate this as "deliver us from the evil one?" Certainly, for all evil comes first from the devil. The world and our own sinful flesh are simply willing to go along with that which opposes God.

It is the devil, ultimately, who obstructs everything for which we pray: that God's name be kept holy, that God's kingdom come, that we receive our daily bread, and that we have a clear conscience.

We pray in this petition that God help us get rid of all misfortune. More-so, knowing that we will be victims in the spiritual battle waged between God and all that is evil, we pray for the faith to hold firmly to Him in times of distress.

Since we live in this world, since, presently, this world is ruled by evil, we can expect poverty, shame, and misery. The devil not only is a liar but a murderer. His is a kingdom of lies and destruction. Though he has been defeated by the death and resurrection of Jesus Christ, he holds power until our Lord comes in victory.

Thus we pray, "Heavenly Father, keep us from all evil, from the snares of the devil, from despair of Your mercy, and from failing to trust You." For without God's continual support, we would not be safe, we could not stand for an instant.

May our Lord grant this petition, giving you the blessings of life everlasting for the sake of Christ Jesus, our Lord. Amen.

08/10/2020 – *But Deliver Us From Evil – Part 3* – Matthew 6:13

Matthew 6:13

> 13 And lead us not into temptation, but deliver us from evil. (ESV)

Although we pray "deliver us from evil," we still are victims of that which opposes the good that God created. Because we live in a sin-sickened world, even because of our own impure desires, we will have problems. Be it a fire, flood, a diagnosis of cancer, or any number of disasters, we pray also for the strength of faith to hold firmly to God's promises when things do not happen for our good.

There are two responses to the evil which happens. First, we can turn away from God, blaming Him for that which is caused by our sin. Otherwise, we can continue to hold firmly to Him, knowing that from the greatest evil, He will create good.

On the night Jesus was betrayed, He prayed that He might be spared from the pain and horror of the crucifixion. "Not my will, but Yours be done," Jesus said. The answer Jesus received was the kiss from Judas, being abandoned by His disciples, the torture and death on the cross.

Yet that evil overcame the power of death, for the grave could not hold the sinless Son of God. Our salvation from sin, death, and the power of the devil is assured because Jesus rose from the dead, showing that He paid the price for our redemption.

When we pray, "deliver us from evil," we pray that God's will be done, that He overcome evil with blessings. This is a prayer of faith, a prayer which places our heavenly Father first, that shows our trust in Him.

May our Lord deliver you from evil, even if that deliverance is the strength to hold firmly to Him when all seems lost. Amen.

08/12/2020 – *For Thine is the Kingdom* – Matthew 6:13

Matthew 6:13

> 13 And lead us not into temptation, but deliver us from evil: For thine is the kingdom, and the power, and the glory, for ever. Amen. (KJV)

One of the arguments against the Bible is the New Testament contains a number of variant readings. This is true. As the copyists listened to the text being read, as they wrote what they heard, they made some spelling mistakes or used the wrong form of a word.

None of the variants matter for doctrine. None of the variants change the message of salvation by grace through faith for the sake of Christ Jesus. Indeed, with a couple of minor exceptions, we can determine the proper reading as we compare the different manuscripts.

One addition, not found in the oldest manuscripts, is the doxology commonly said at the end of the Lord's Prayer. It may have been added to a manuscript copy by a scribe familiar with the early Christian book, the *Didache*.

Those who translated the New Testament from Greek to English at the time of King James had a manuscript with this doxology, "For Thine is the kingdom and the power and the glory forever and ever. Amen." Thus the ending came in to use in English speaking countries which used the King James Version.

Does this change the validity of the prayer? Not in the least. Our heavenly Father still hears our prayer, even if the doxology may have come from a source other than Matthew or Luke, who quoted Jesus' words.

We boldly pray, therefore, as Jesus taught His disciples. knowing that our Father hears our prayers. Amen.

08/14/2020 – *Amen* – Matthew 6:13

Matthew 6:13

> 13 And lead us not into temptation, but deliver us from evil: For thine is the kingdom, and the power, and the glory, for ever. Amen. (KJV)

It is not uncommon for a word in one language to be used in another. Examples abound where French, Latin, German, or Spanish words are in common use in our daily conversations. So it is with the Hebrew word, *amen*.

There are several ways which we use the word *amen*. The first is to show our agreement with a statement, often to voice that a public prayer offered by a pastor is a prayer that we, too, and utter. Therefore we intone, "amen," giving our voice to that of the person praying. If we disagree with the prayer, we remain silent, not showing agreement. No one can demand that you say "amen" when you find the prayer offensive in some manner.

The other use is to proclaim that something is true, that we trust that which we have heard. Jesus preceded a number of lessons by saying, "Amen, amen, I say to you." In this way He alerted His disciples, and us, that He indeed speaks the truth.

As Christians, we also use the word "amen" to show that what is heard is the truth. We can relate to people saying "amen" when they receive absolution for their sins.

When we pray, when we conclude the prayer with "amen," we are showing both agreement with the content of the prayer, expressing the truth of the prayer, and showing faith that God will hear and answer our prayer. In so doing, we are joining with the faithful from the earliest days of the Old Testament to the faithful of today.

What a great privilege to use this word. This is most certainly true. Amen.

08/17/2020 – *With the Lord Begin Your Task – Part 1* – Colossians 3:17

Colossians 3:17

> 17 And whatever you do, in word or deed, do everything in the name of the Lord Jesus, giving thanks to God the Father through him. (ESV)

When Jesus said, "Seek first the kingdom of God and His righteousness,"[29] Matthew 6:33 He reminds us that all we do reflects our faith in Him as our redeemer. Christians cannot simply gather on Sunday, only to ignore God for the rest of the week. Every day, every task, is an opportunity to dedicate our lives to God's service.

There is an old German hymn which shows up in several Lutheran hymnals, "With the Lord Begin Your Task." It speaks of our priority, that no matter how insignificant the project, we should begin with prayer. Saint Paul admonished the Colossian Christians, "And whatever you do, in word or deed, do everything in the name of the Lord Jesus, giving thanks to God the Father through him." This advice puts all we do into proper perspective.

No matter how seemingly insignificant our job, if we are going to take the time to accomplish something, it is worthwhile. Luther's concept of vocation says that the young mother changing a dirty diaper is doing a deed which is praise-worthy. Her simple act of serving her child in need is serving God, Himself.

Thus we can start our day with this hymn[30] LSB 869, *With the Lord Begin Your Task*, vs. 1

```
With the Lord begin your task; Jesus will direct it.
For His aid and counsel ask; Jesus will perfect it.
Every morn with Jesus rise, and when day is ended,
In His name then close your eyes; Be to Him commended.
```

May our Lord be with you in all things this day. Amen.

---

[29] Matthew 6:33a
[30] .

08/19/2020 – *With the Lord Begin Your Task – Part 2* – Colossians 3:17

Colossians 3:17

> 17 And whatever you do, in word or deed, do everything in the name of the Lord Jesus, giving thanks to God the Father through him. (ESV)

Martin Luther dealt with practical theology. He was most concerned with individuals knowing the grace of God, that we are saved from sin, death, and the power of the devil by the sacrifice of Jesus Christ on the cross of Calvary. Jesus' resurrection shows His victory over death and the grave, assuring us that we, too, shall rise again.

Practical theology teaches a way of life which gives glory to God while accomplishing those day-to-day things that we must do. Saint Paul, also giving practical advice, wrote: "And whatever you do, in word or deed, do everything in the name of the Lord Jesus, giving thanks to God the Father through him."

From the viewpoint of practical theology, let's discover what the anonymous hymn writer suggested in the hymn, "With the Lord Begin Your Task."[31]

> Let each day begin with prayer, Praise, and adoration.
> On the Lord cast every care; He is your salvation,
> Morning, evening, and at night Jesus will be near you,
> Save you from the tempter's might, With His presence cheer you.

May our Lord grant you the wisdom to begin and end each day in prayer, commending all you do to Him. Amen.

---

[31] LSB 869, *With the Lord Begin Your Task*, vs. 2

08/21/2020 – *With the Lord Begin Your Task* – Part 3 – Colossians 3:17

Colossians 3:17

> 17 And whatever you do, in word or deed, do everything in the name of the Lord Jesus, giving thanks to God the Father through him. (ESV)

Because we follow Saint Paul's admonition, "And whatever you do, in word or deed, do everything in the name of the Lord Jesus, giving thanks to God the Father through him," we commend all our daily tasks to Christ Jesus. This does not mean that we will never have trouble, for this sinful world fights God's good and gracious will. But, in beginning and ending each day, each task, with prayer, we know that our Lord blesses our efforts.

Things are going to go wrong. Our plans may fail. We may have setbacks, yet those setbacks inevitably turn out to be blessings. By beginning and ending with prayer, we say "Thy will be done," trusting in God's grace and mercy to bless all that we do.

Even as things do not go according to plan, we can sing with the anonymous German hymn writer[32] LSB 869, *With the Lord Begin Your Task*, vs 3

```
With your Savior at your side, Foes need not alarm you;
In His promises confide, And no ill can harm you.
All your trust and hope repose In the mighty Master,
Who in wisdom truly knows How to stem disaster.
```

Thus we rely on Jesus' promise, "I am with you until the end of the age." In all things, even if we are having a bad day, He is our rock and our salvation. May our Lord comfort you with these words. Amen.

---

[32]:

08/24/2020 – *With the Lord Begin Your Task – Part 4* – Colossians 3:17

Colossians 3:17

> 17 And whatever you do, in word or deed, do everything in the name of the Lord Jesus, giving thanks to God the Father through him. (ESV)

Part of resilience, being able to bounce back from the changes and chances of life, is keeping a matter of perspective. The big picture says that we are saved by God's rich love as shown to us through the death and resurrection of Jesus Christ. Although we have sinned, Jesus took upon Himself our sin, giving to us His righteousness. Thus we look beyond our present troubles, keeping our eyes on Jesus, the author and perfecter of our faith.

As ones who trust first in God, we agree with Saint Paul: "And whatever you do, in word or deed, do everything in the name of the Lord Jesus, giving thanks to God the Father through him." Our efforts lead to good for our neighbor, even if we learn by failing and restarting. We give glory to God, and trust in Him for all blessings, including the strength, stamina, and desire to serve Him by serving our neighbor.

The anonymous German hymn writer reminds us[33] LSB 869, *With the Lord Begin Your Task*, vs 4

```
    If your task be thus begun, With the Savior's blessing,
  Safely then your course will run, Toward the promise pressing.
  Good will follow everywhere While you here must wander;
  You at last the joy will share In the mansions yonder.
```

May our Lord bless you this day as you do His work, serving Him by serving your neighbors, your family, and all around you. Amen.

---

[33].

08/26/2020 – *With the Lord Begin Your Task* – Part 5 – Colossians 3:17

Colossians 3:17

> 17 And whatever you do, in word or deed, do everything in the name of the Lord Jesus, giving thanks to God the Father through him. (ESV)

Our anonymous German hymn writer reminds us that we begin and end all we do with prayer. This becomes habitual as we seek first the kingdom of God and His righteousness. Saint Paul calls upon us: "And whatever you do, in word or deed, do everything in the name of the Lord Jesus, giving thanks to God the Father through him."

Our first thought at the beginning of the day is thanksgiving that God has given us a new morning in which to live in His grace and mercy. Our last thought at the end of the night is we are forgiven all our sins for the sake of Christ Jesus, that we have the promise of life everlasting.

We are bold to sing[34] LSB 869, *With the Lord Begin Your Task*, vs 5

```
Thus, Lord Jesus, every task Be to You commended;
May Your will be done, I ask, Until life is ended.
Jesus, in Your name begun Be the day's endeavor;
Grant that it may well be done To Your praise forever.
```

May our Lord continue to be with you and bless you this day in whatever you may do. To Him be the glory. Amen.

---

[34].

08/28/2020 – *Seek First* – Part 1 – Matthew 6:33

Matthew 6:33

> 33 But seek first the kingdom of God and his righteousness, and all these things will be added to you. (ESV)

In the next few weeks we are going to look at the Beatitudes, the beginning of Jesus' *Sermon on the Mount.* Throughout the study we will consider two main truths. The first, the Kingdom of God presents a paradox in this world. The second, as Christians we are admonished to seek first the Kingdom of God and His righteousness. Everything else is of less importance.

What is this kingdom of God for which we seek? It is nothing less than the Gospel, that Jesus Christ died to pay the price of our sins. He comes to us with this forgiveness through the proclaimed Word of God and through the properly administered sacraments.

To seek the kingdom of God we first confess that we are sinful and unclean, that we are born in sin, and live in sin, and deserve to die eternally because of our sin. That sin can be our actions against God and neighbor, it can be inaction against the same. That sin can be in our secret thoughts, in our words, or in our actions. When we cause harm, either by our works or by our refusal to assist, we have transgressed the law of God.

But Jesus Christ redeemed us from the guilt of sin. For His sake we are declared holy and righteous in God's sight. This is not because of our good works, or anything within us that is good, but purely by God's love, grace, and mercy.

This grace is what we seek. This grace gives us peace in this sin-sickened world. This grace gives us the hope of life everlasting for the sake of Christ Jesus. This grace is the kingdom of God.

May our Lord grant you His grace and favor as You seek Him above all things. Amen.

08/31/2020 – *Seek First* – Part 2 – Matthew 6:33

Matthew 6:33

> 33 But seek first the kingdom of God and his righteousness, and all these things will be added to you. (ESV)

We have been looking at the kingdom of God, as Jesus admonished, "But seek first the kingdom of God." The kingdom of God is the righteousness of Jesus Christ credited to us by God the Father for the sake of the bitter suffering and death of Jesus Christ. He makes us members of His kingdom, with all rights and privileges of citizenship in heaven, out of His great love and mercy. You and I do nothing to earn this right to call God our heavenly Father.

Although the kingdom of heaven seeks us through the working of the Holy Spirit, as members of the kingdom we seek to learn more about God's rich grace. Our desire is to better understand such a love that the Father has that we should be called His beloved children.

Where is the kingdom to be found? In God's holy and inspired Word. It is through the Word and the sacraments, the Word of promise joined with the physical elements of water, of bread and wine, by which faith is given so we can hold firmly to His promises.

We seek the kingdom of God in daily devotions, in Bible study, in attending church, in receiving the message of the Gospel. We seek the kingdom of God by living daily as His dear children, giving Him honor in all that we do.

May our Lord grant you the wisdom to seek His kingdom, to trust always in His promises. Amen.

09/02/2020 – *Seek First – Part 3* – Matthew 6:33

Matthew 6:33

> 33 But seek first the kingdom of God and his righteousness, and all these things will be added to you. (ESV)

Jesus said, "But seek first the kingdom of God and His righteousness." The Holy Spirit makes us members of God's kingdom through the proclaimed Gospel and the Word joined with the visible elements of water, bread, and wine in the sacraments. God declares us holy in His sight through the words of absolution, where He forgives us our sins against both God and neighbor.

How does a citizen of the kingdom of God act? Are we not also citizens of this world? Is there something to set us apart?

Indeed, because we are of God's kingdom, because we have received His undeserved love, we act in a way the world does not understand. Although God does not need our good works, our neighbor does. We give glory to God by serving those around us, caring for their spiritual, emotional, and physical needs. As ones who have received grace, we reflect that grace in love towards both God and neighbor.

For the most part, the good we do for those around us is not premeditated, and may actually be invisible to us. It may be the simple, cheerful "hello" spoken to a stranger, or holding the door for someone, or letting a person cut in line at the grocery store. These things we do, not thinking, but simply because we seek the good of those around us.

Our good works, especially the ones of which we are ignorant, show God's love for all people. You and I are His hands, the ones entrusted with the care of each person around us.

May our Lord richly bless you as you serve Him by reflecting His love to this confused world. Amen.

09/04/2020 – *Seek First – Part 4* – Matthew 6:33

Matthew 6:33

> 33 But seek first the kingdom of God and his righteousness, and all these things will be added to you. (ESV)

The kingdom of God is a paradox. What we expect from the Creator is not what we see. An absolute monarch demands obedience and service from his subjects. One who is a leader takes that which is best, leaving the rest for her subjects. The IRS takes from the top of our paycheck, no matter our desires, because we are subject to the laws and whims of the government.

Not so with the kingdom of God. Jesus said, "But seek first the kingdom of God and his righteousness, and all these things will be added to you." He was admonishing His disciples not to worry about the things of this world, about power, about clothing, about shelter, about food. God provides, our worry does not help. He gives us that which we need to sustain our body and life.

To seek God's kingdom is to rely on His Word, to trust in His promises. Through the gift of faith we fix our eyes on Jesus, trusting in God's mercy to care for us eternally. The transient nature of this world pales in comparison with the joys of eternity.

We seek God's kingdom, daily studying His word, meditating on His promises as we do those things which serve our families, our friends, and those strangers we are so fortunate to meet. In so doing, we find greater satisfaction than if we selfishly looked only for our own benefit. This is one paradox of being a Christian.

May our Lord enable you to seek first His kingdom, to know His love, grace, and mercy, and to draw comfort from His sacrifice for you. Amen.

09/07/2020 – *Seek First* – Part 5 – Matthew 6:33

Matthew 6:33

> 33 But seek first the kingdom of God and his righteousness, and all these things will be added to you. (ESV)

Jesus said, "But seek first the kingdom of God and his righteousness, and all these things will be added to you." The kingdom of God is a paradox. We seek first the kingdom of God, not to receive the things of this life, but because we understand that, as precious as this world is to us, the promise of everlasting life because of Jesus Christ is much greater. "I am but a stranger here, heaven is my home," says an old hymn. It properly shows our priorities.

As we seek first God's kingdom rather than our own glory or benefit, our priorities change. We begin to realize that many of the goodies which the world demands we obtain are, in fact, without value. What good is the 60-inch television when that which is broadcast is of such little value? What good is the mansion when we realize our possessions own us more than we own them?

True contentment comes in serving others because God first served us by sending Christ Jesus to redeem us from sin, death, and the emptiness of this world. Rust and decay, the second law of entropy, are our lot in this life. God's rich favor is our lot in His kingdom. The eternal blessedness of seeing Him face to face shows us the vacuousness of the world.

Thus a paradox. By using what we have for the good of others, by supporting various charities and worthy causes, we actually gain in the intangible blessings of life. By showing love, we receive love in return, in abundance. In serving our neighbor because God has loved us, we are in fact serving Him.

May you find joy in seeking first the kingdom of God. May you find peace in relying on God's rich promises of life eternal for the sake of Christ Jesus, our Lord. Amen.

09/09/2020 – *Blessed are the Poor in Spirit – Part 1* – Matthew 5:3

Matthew 5:3

> 3 Blessed are the poor in spirit, for theirs is the kingdom of heaven. (ESV)

Early in Jesus' ministry He took His disciples and followers up a mountain so to teach them about the kingdom of God. To set the tone of this discourse, Jesus began by explaining who are blessed in the kingdom. "Blessed are the poor in spirit, for theirs is the kingdom of heaven."

Immediately we run into a paradox. Why are the poor in spirit blessed? What makes them poor in spirit?

Those who rely on themselves, those who are strong in their belief that their works, their knowledge, their strength will earn them a place in the kingdom of God will be sorely disappointed. Saint Luke told of two men who went into the Temple to pray, a Pharisee and a tax collector. The Pharisee told God everything he did right. The Pharisee left, secure in his self-righteousness but unforgiven. The tax collector, in shame, said, "Lord, be merciful to me, the sinner." He received forgiveness.

The poor in spirit recognize that they cannot, by their own reason or strength, enter the kingdom of God. They cannot save themselves. They trust only in the merits of Jesus Christ, who sacrificed Himself on the cross so that they might have eternal life.

The poor in spirit know that salvation is by grace through faith for the sake of Christ. The faith which holds to God's promises is the gift of God given through Word and sacrament by the working of the Holy Spirit. To be poor in spirit is to trust in God alone, to seek first His kingdom and righteousness.

"Blessed are the poor in spirit, for theirs is the kingdom of heaven." Amen.

09/11/2020 – *Blessed are the Poor in Spirit – Part 2* – Matthew 5:3

Matthew 5:3

3 Blessed are the poor in spirit, for theirs is the kingdom of heaven. (ESV)

Jesus said, "Blessed are the poor in spirit, for theirs is the kingdom of heaven."

Our confirmands, as part of their studies, memorize Luther's *Small Catechism*. In so doing, they both learn the basics of the Christian faith, and they have a ready answer for questions which may arise as they discuss Christianity.

Martin Luther told what it means to be poor in spirit as he explained the Third Article of the Apostles' Creed:

> I believe that I cannot, by my own reason or strength, believe in Jesus Christ, my Lord or come to Him; But the Holy Spirit has called me by the Gospel, enlightened me with His gifts, sanctified and kept me in the true faith.

Only the poor in spirit, the ones who rely, in faith, on God's rich grace, can truly make this confession. In such a confession is the strength of the Triune God, a strength which overcomes the devil, the world, and our own sinful flesh. Thus the paradox, in our weakness we are given God's strength. To Him be the glory.

"Blessed are the poor in spirit, for theirs is the kingdom of heaven." Amen.

09/14/2020 – *Blessed are They that Mourn, for They Shall be Comforted – Part 1* – Matthew 5:4

Matthew 5:4

4 Blessed are those who mourn, for they shall be comforted. (ESV)

Jesus said, "Blessed are those who mourn, for they shall be comforted." The paradox of Christianity continues.

There are two ways to look at this blessing. The first, those who mourn over lost loved ones will be comforted. This would be the Christians encouraged by Saint Paul,

> But we do not want you to be uninformed, brothers, about those who are asleep, that you may not grieve as others do who have no hope.[35] 1 Thessalonians 4:13

While we mourn for our loss, we have the comfort of God's rich promise of life everlasting. Those who precede us into heaven are even now experiencing the joy of seeing God face to face, of the reality that in all things they are blessed. We rejoice for them, and long to be with them.

We find comfort in the Lord's Supper, when we hear, in the Proper Preface, "Therefore with angels and archangels and all the company of heaven," knowing that we are joined with all the saints as they sing God's praise.

The world may see death as the end. Christians see death as the doorway to heaven. The world may see death as a reward for good works, though the world never says "You have done enough." Christian see death as Christ Jesus saying, "I have redeemed you, now enter into your eternal rest in my loving arms."

Thus, "Blessed are those who mourn, for they shall be comforted." Amen.

---

[35] 1 Thessalonians 4:13 (ESV)

09/16/2020 – *Blessed are They that Mourn, for They Shall be Comforted – Part 2* – Matthew 5:4

Matthew 5:4

> 4 Blessed are those who mourn, for they shall be comforted. (ESV)

Jesus said, "Blessed are those who mourn, for they shall be comforted." We looked at the teaching that those who mourn over lost loved ones will be comforted. Many Christian commentators, while accepting this idea, also suggest that those who mourn over their sin shall be comforted.

The Bible is split into two main doctrines, the law and the Gospel. The purpose of the law is to accuse us of our sin. Where Saint Paul said, "The wages of sin is death,"[36] Romans 6:23 he brought the full weight of the law on sinners. God does not grade on the curve, God does not ignore the most insignificant sin.

When confronted by the law, if we are honest with ourselves, we can only say, "I have sinned and fallen short of the glory of God. I have no hope in myself." Thus we mourn our sin, knowing that we deserve to be removed from God's sight eternally.

Paul continued, "But the free gift of God is eternal life in Christ Jesus our Lord." What sweet comfort this promise gives. For the sake of His innocent suffering and death, we have life everlasting. We are assured of God's promise of grace and mercy.

Is it any wonder, then, that Jesus said, "Blessed are those who mourn, for they shall be comforted?" Amen.

---

[36] Romans 6:23

09/18/2020 – *Blessed are the Meek* – Part 1 – Matthew 5:5

Matthew 5:5

> 4 Blessed are the meek, for they shall inherit the earth. (ESV)

Christianity is full of paradoxes. The One through whom everything was created was an infant, suffered, died, and rose again to serve His creation. We are at the same time completely a sinner yet completely a saint. The meek, not the strong, shall inherit the earth.

What does Jesus mean? Is this looking forward to heaven, or does it have practical application while we still are living today? Don't the strong, don't the powerful make all the decisions and get all of the glory?

The meek are those who are willing to suffer wrong, who do not insist on all of their rights, but are willing to step aside for the good of their neighbor. Rather than seeking revenge, they look for ways to help those who have caused them harm. Rather than looking to obtain everything due, they are generous.

It is true that this is not the way to great wealth, to mansions, to untold fame. It is, however, the way to contentment, peace, and security. It is the result of trusting in God, of seeking His kingdom and His righteousness rather than our own benefit.

Being meek, looking for the good of others, holding firmly in faith to God's grace rather than our own strength, is truly a blessing. "Blessed are the meek, for they shall inherit the earth." Amen.

09/21/2020 – *Blessed are the Meek – Part 2* – Matthew 5:5

Matthew 5:5

    4 Blessed are the meek, for they shall inherit the earth. (ESV)

Jesus said, "Blessed are the meek, for they shall inherit the earth." In our personal lives, this is truly a blessing. However, there are times when we must stand up for those entrusted to our care.

Luther noted that those who rule, who have the power of government, cannot be meek. God gives them the power of the sword, the power to enforce laws even to the point of capital punishment. Parents must be parents, not meek in raising their children, for the good of the family. In the way, teachers must maintain discipline in the classroom, and business owners must be strong in their stewardship of their businesses.

Yet in our dealings with others, we see them as ones for whom Christ Jesus died. If we look at the world with the eyes of Jesus, we look with love, with the desire that they receive the care and consideration due each person.

"Blessed are the meek, for they shall inherit the earth." May our Lord bless you in your efforts to treat His creation with love and respect, to His glory. Amen.

09/22/2020 – *Blessed are Those Who Hunger and Thirst – Part 1* – Matthew 5:6

Matthew 5:6

> 6 Blessed are those who hunger and thirst for righteousness, for they shall be satisfied. (ESV)

As we continue looking at the Beatitudes, we come to those who hunger and thirst for righteousness. Before we discuss the longing for righteousness, let's begin with defining the word.

To be righteous is to act in accordance with God's law and His holy will. Simply put, it is loving God with your whole heart, mind, and soul. It is also loving your neighbor as yourself.

We fail in our quest to be righteous. Even as we try to do that which is right, we end up sinning against God and man.

Yet, we are declared righteous by God for the sake of the suffering and death of Jesus Christ. In the Beatitudes, the sense of the word righteousness is not our actions, but the grace of God given to us. Those who have faith in Christ Jesus as their Savior from sin and death have been granted the verdict of righteousness.

"Blessed are those who hunger and thirst for righteousness, for they shall be satisfied." Amen.

09/23/2020 – *Blessed are Those Who Hunger and Thirst – Part 2* – Matthew 5:6

Matthew 5:6

> 6 Blessed are those who hunger and thirst for righteousness, for they shall be satisfied. (ESV)

The Psalmist wrote, "My soul thirsts for God, for the living God."[37] Psalms 42:2 Isaiah wrote, "Come, everyone who thirsts, come to the waters."[38] Isaiah 55:1 Jesus told the woman at the well of Sychar that He is the living water.[39] John 4:7–26

On a hot summer day, when working outside, nothing sounds as refreshing as a cold drink. Ice water tastes better than the best wine when thirst rages. Old beer commercials speak of the reward of a refreshing beverage after a difficult job is completed.

Those who truly understand that they are sinful, that they cannot by their own actions redeem themselves, have that type of thirst and desire to be declared righteous in God's sight. Their thirst is quenched by the living water, Jesus Christ, Himself, who bore their sins on the cross. Daily, as we confess our sins to God, we are assured of being forgiven. We are refreshed, knowing that the forgiveness of sins brings to us life everlasting.

"Blessed are those who hunger and thirst for righteousness, for they shall be satisfied." Amen.

---

[37] Psalm 42:2
[38] Isaiah 55:1
[39] John 4:7-26

09/24/2020 – *Blessed are the Merciful* – Part 1 – Matthew 5:7

Matthew 5:7

> 7 Blessed are the merciful, for they shall receive mercy. (ESV)

One would be hard-pressed not to know of the riots, looting, and general destruction happening in our larger cities. Minneapolis has had several bouts of riots, where whole neighborhoods are destroyed in the name of justice. Even little Kenosha, Wisconsin, has seen death and destruction as people seek restitution and redress for perceived wrongs.

Martin Luther wrote,

> For that is one of the virtues of sham sanctity that it can have no compassion for or mercy upon the fallible and weak, but insists upon the extremest strictness and most careful selection, and as soon as there is the slightest failure, all mercy is gone and they do nothing but fume and fret; as also St. Gregory shows how to recognize this, and say: ... "true holiness is merciful and compassionate, but false holiness can do nothing but be angry and rage;" and yet they say: ... we do it through love and zeal for righteousness.[40]

The rioters show little mercy for the businesses they loot, the families they force into the street as houses burn, the first responders who are injured for trying to serve their communities.

There is a better way. We will be looking at Jesus' words, "Blessed are the merciful, for they shall receive mercy." We will come to know that, as God shows mercy, so we, too, can be merciful. Until then, may our Lord grant you peace. Amen.

---

[40] Luther's Works, American Edition, vol 21, p. 29

09/25/2020 – *Blessed are the Merciful – Part 2* – Matthew 5:7

Matthew 5:7

> 7 Blessed are the merciful, for they shall receive mercy. (ESV)

What is this mercy of which Jesus speaks? It is the willingness to help others, to seek their good, to bind their wounds, to care for their needs. When the merciful see pain, misery, and distress, they show love and compassion.

We think of the volunteers in the Red Cross who drop everything to go to the Gulf Coast to set up shelters for victims of the hurricanes. These same volunteers stand with families who have lost their homes to fire or flood. There are the Hospice volunteers who seek to make the last days of strangers comfortable, or the Civil Air Patrol volunteers who spend their time looking for the lost.

These are acts of mercy. More often than not, those who demonstrate such selfless mercy are found in the pews at church. They have received the full pardon of their sins, not because of their works, but because of God's love.

As ones who have experienced mercy, they desire to pass that mercy to others. Thus we see that mercy shown again and again, both in small acts of kindness, is sacrificial giving of time and talent, and even in founding organizations such as hospitals, nursing homes, and other institutions where the sick, the sorrowful, and the dying may find relief.

"Blessed are the merciful, for they shall receive mercy." Amen.

09/28/2020 – *Blessed are the Merciful – Part 3* – Matthew 5:7

Matthew 5:7

7 Blessed are the merciful, for they shall receive mercy. (ESV)

We have been looking at the acts of mercy which flow from the forgiveness of sins, from being declared holy in God's sight for the sake of the death and resurrection of Jesus Christ. Indeed these acts of mercy are the fruits of faith, the proof that faith is living. Yet there is more to mercy than loving our neighbors as ourselves.

The sad truth is, as long as we live in this sinful world, we will be sinned against. People will speak ill of us, lie about us, and look to cause us harm. We can retaliate, but that serves no one, as the riots in our cities unfortunately demonstrate once again.

We have been forgiven, our sins covered by the righteousness of Jesus Christ. Therefore, we can forgive. God gives us a heart of love which understands the fleeting nature of this life. As the Reformation hymn says, "Take they our life; goods, fame, child, and wife; though these all be gone, they yet have nothing won. The kingdom ours remaineth."[41]

Because those who sin against us do us no lasting harm, there is no reason to hold a grudge, to retain forgiveness. We truly have the ability, through God's mercy, to show mercy at all times.

"Blessed are the merciful, for they shall receive mercy." Amen.

---

[41] A Mighty Fortress, vs 4

09/29/2020 – *Blessed are the Merciful – Part 4* – Matthew 5:7

Matthew 5:7

> 7 Blessed are the merciful, for they shall receive mercy. (ESV)

Those who show mercy, those who reflect the love of Christ Jesus, do so without the thought of reward. God gives them the ability to show compassion and forgiveness, for this is not the natural state of any human. Yet, Jesus here gives a promise.

The mercy which the merciful receive is not a heavenly reward. There is no misery in heaven, no want, no hatred, no need to be given mercy. Those in heaven are there because of God's mercy, but there is no need of comfort or forgiveness in the house of God. There is no sin.

Thus, the merciful have the promise of receiving mercy here on earth. God first makes us merciful, then He blesses us for being merciful. It is His work in and through us, yet He richly blesses us as we do His will.

That blessing may come from the satisfaction of helping one another. That blessing may come from the comfort of knowing you have forgiven as you are forgiven. That blessing may be a physical reward. All we know, God richly blesses those who reflect His mercy and grace.

May our Lord richly bless you as He uses you to show His love, grace, favor, and mercy in this sin-darkened world. May you find peace in His mercy.

"Blessed are the merciful, for they shall receive mercy." Amen.

09/30/2020 – *Blessed are the Pure in Heart* – Part 1 – Matthew 5:8

Matthew 5:8

8 Blessed are the pure in heart, for they shall see God. (ESV)

The first four Beatitudes spoke of the relationship between God and man. The next three speak of our relationship with our neighbor. We have looked at the quality of mercy, that our good works reflect that we have received the forgiveness of sins for the sake of Christ Jesus.

Now Jesus tells us, "Blessed are the pure in heart, for they shall see God."

What does this mean? Are the pure in heart those who do good works, those who are seen by one and all as being more holy and pious than the crowds? That was the view of the Pharisees in the time of Christ, counterparts we see today in both the church and society. No, it is not our religious piety or our good intentions.

Are the pure in heart the morals police, the ones who seek to prohibit people from having certain experiences, or being exposed to various pieces of art? The church does not exist to demand moral behavior; moral behavior comes from knowing our sins are forgiven, that we reflect God's grace and mercy. Yes, pornography ruins lives, the misuse of various substances such as alcohol or tobacco can shorten our time on earth. But the church does not demand a certain outward life, though the church rejoices when members act responsibly for their own good.

The pure in heart is one who is honest, who has no hidden motive, no selfish interest, and is open in all things. The pure in heart is one who is given that gift by God.

"Blessed are the pure in heart, for they shall see God." Amen.

10/01/2020 – *Blessed are the Pure in Heart – Part 1* – Matthew 5:8

Matthew 5:8

> 8 Blessed are the pure in heart, for they shall see God. (ESV)

The pure in heart are such because of the gift of God. It is not something we accomplish by our good works, our desires, or our own strength. It is the gift of faith, that gift of God which holds firmly to His promises of grace and mercy.

The pure in heart seeks first the kingdom of God and His righteousness. The pure in heart ponders God's Word as it applies to himself, to herself. The pure in heart stands under God's love, forgiven of all sins, holy in God's sight.

Saint Paul wrote to Titus: "To the pure, all things are pure, but to the defiled and unbelieving, nothing is pure; but both their minds and their consciences are defiled."[42] Titus 1:15 Thus, in all things those who are pure in heart walk in the grace of God. Their lives reflect God's goodness. Their hearts accept that which God offers, namely the forgiveness of sins for Christ's sake, which leads to life everlasting.

Here the pure in heart see God dimly through the Gospel and sacraments. Soon, however, they will be taken by all God's angels to behold Him face to face, knowing fully His love and mercy. May our Lord grant you peace as you are declared righteous in His sight because of the death and resurrection of Jesus.

"Blessed are the pure in heart, for they shall see God." Amen.

---

[42] Titus 1:15 (ESV)

10/02/2020 – *Blessed are the Peacemakers* – Matthew 5:9

Matthew 5:9

> 9 Blessed are the peacemakers, for they shall be called sons of God. (ESV)

The peace of God is the sure and certain hope of life everlasting through Jesus Christ. Those who are filled with this peace, those who are saved by God's great love through faith in the atonement given because Jesus died for their sins, reflect that peace. They live in peace, if at all possible. They work to restore peace, if at all possible, when those of this world seek harm and vengeance.

However, this is not peace at any price, which ignores the truth of Christian doctrine, the truth of the natural laws set up by God as He created the heavens and the earth. This is the peace which comes from loving God with our whole heart, soul, and mind; and loving our neighbor as ourselves. It is the love that weeps over the lost, over those who live in the darkness of sin, in the delusion of some lie espoused by this world.

In the world, where strife arises, the faithful peacemakers work for peace in the same way Jesus worked to reconcile us to the Father. This sacrificial love seeks to reconcile those in conflict in the same way that Jesus, out of His love, gave Himself to pay the price of our sin.

Is it any wonder, then, that God bestows on them the name "sons of God?" They reflect His love, His grace, His mercy, His peace, even as they desire the good of all people.

May our Lord grant you the peace of knowing your sins are forgiven for the sake of Jesus, and that you reflect His love in this world.

"Blessed are the peacemakers, for they shall be called sons of God." Amen

10/05/2020 – *Blessed are the Persecuted – Part 1* – Matthew 5:10

Matthew 5:10

> 10 Blessed are you when others revile you and persecute you and utter all kinds of evil against you falsely on my account. (ESV)

Throughout this study of the Beatitudes we have looked at the paradox of being a Christian. Blessed are the poor in spirit, blessed are they that mourn, blessed are the meek. This goes against the grain, against common sense.

Christians are in the world, not of the world. They seek first God's kingdom and His righteousness, leaving the earthly goodies for someone else. Unlike those who believe this world is all there is, Christians are highly aware of the temporary nature of things. The flashy new car eventually wears out, clothing gets soiled and torn, even our bodies weaken as we grow older.

Those who seek first the wealth and wisdom of this world tend not to like people who are different. All sorts of discrimination happens with people who do not fit the norms of a given time and place. In the past people of color were looked upon as being subhuman, while today one of the world's major religions indiscriminately kills because people disagree with their world view.

Yet Christians are blessed, not in this world, certainly, with being falsely accused. This means their lives reflect God's love, not the hatred of this world. They are different, their very lives give witness to the lies of this world.

"Blessed are you when others revile you and persecute you and utter all kinds of evil against you falsely on my account." Amen

10/06/2020 – *Blessed are the Persecuted – Part 2* – Matthew 5:10

Matthew 5:10

> 10 Blessed are you when others revile you and persecute you and utter all kinds of evil against you falsely on my account. (ESV)

We are used to advertising hype, the half-truths told to sell products. Buy the right dietary supplement, and the pounds will melt off while you sleep. Drive the right car and everyone will marvel at your success. Wear the right clothing and you will achieve complete happiness. When you get the product home, you still need to lose the weight, your car looks like most others on the road, and you still are unhappy with the fit of the jacket.

Jesus never made claims that Christians would have an easy time in this life. On the night He was betrayed, He told His disciples:

> If the world hates you, know that it has hated me before it hated you. If you were of the world, the world would love you as its own; but because you are not of the world, but I chose you out of the world, therefore the world hates you.[43] John 15:18–19

Our job description includes slander, persecution, and even death. Yet we are blessed when so persecuted, for this shows we are not of this world. It is the paradox of being a Christian, even as Jesus taught His disciples while giving them the Beatitudes. We are blessed because of God's rich love, His grace which saves us from sin and death.

"Blessed are you when others revile you and persecute you and utter all kinds of evil against you falsely on my account." Amen

---

[43] John 15:18-19 (ESV)

10/07/2020 – *Blessed are the Persecuted – Part 3* – Matthew 5:10

Matthew 5:10

> 10 Blessed are you when others revile you and persecute you and utter all kinds of evil against you falsely on my account. (ESV)

The blessings Christians receive because they are reviled and persecuted by this world are not tied to the lies told about them. We believe, teach, and confess that we are involved in spiritual warfare with the devil, the world, and our own sinful flesh. Each of these would have us deny our faith that Jesus Christ is our redeemer from sin and death, that we have life everlasting because of God's rich and undeserved love.

Those who are persecuted, reviled, and slandered because of their faith in Jesus Christ will dwell eternally in the mansions He has prepared only because of faith in Jesus. The works which call forth jealousy, contention, and persecution are fruits of faith. Good works, the fruits of faith, the love shown by Christians to their neighbors, merely are proof that they believe in Jesus Christ as their Savior.

That Christians are persecuted shows that the world rejects the message of God's grace which they bring. Unable to tolerate the Gospel, that Jesus Christ bore the sins of the whole world upon the cross, they seek to silence the messenger. As Martin Luther wrote, "Take they our life; goods, fame, child, and wife; though these all be gone, they yet have nothing won. The kingdom ours remaineth."

"Blessed are you when others revile you and persecute you and utter all kinds of evil against you falsely on my account." Amen

10/08/2020 – *Blessed are You When Persecuted – Part 1* – Matthew 5:11–12

Matthew 5:11–12

> 11 Blessed are you when others revile you and persecute you and utter all kinds of evil against you falsely on my account. Rejoice and be glad, for your reward is great in heaven, for so they persecuted the prophets who were before you. (ESV)

We come to the end of the Beatitudes. In the past few days we looked generally at the lot of the faithful Christian. They can look forward to being outcast by this world, even as they seek to serve God by serving their neighbors. The world would rather destroy those who are different than to accept their loving service.

Now Jesus turns to His disciples, "Blessed are you when others revile you and utter all kinds of evil against you falsely on my account." This becomes personal. Every faithful disciple of Jesus, except John the Evangelist, was martyred for their faith. Every one was willing to die rather than to deny God's rich grace, love, and mercy.

Think about this. Not only the eyewitnesses of Jesus' life on earth willingly went to the grave for proclaiming His death and resurrection, but modern martyrs continue to die for the same truth. We can willingly suffer for our faith, knowing that we are eternally blessed because Jesus died and rose again to redeem us from sin, death, and the power of the devil.

"Blessed are you when others revile you and persecute you and utter all kinds of evil against you falsely on my account. Rejoice and be glad, for your reward is great in heaven, for so they persecuted the prophets who were before you." Amen

10/09/2020 – *Blessed are You When Persecuted – Part 2* – Matthew 5:11–12

Matthew 5:11–12

> 11 Blessed are you when others revile you and persecute you and utter all kinds of evil against you falsely on my account.
>
> 12 Rejoice and be glad, for your reward is great in heaven, for so they persecuted the prophets who were before you. (ESV)

We have come to the end of the Beatitudes. The paradox of being a Christian is clear. That which the world expects is of no value. That which is despised by the world is precious in God's sight.

This is nothing new. Cain killed Abel because Abel's sacrifice made in faith was accepted, while Cain's made as an informal gesture was rejected. Old Testament prophets were rejected because they called the people to repent, to turn from false gods and live. Jesus was crucified because He spoke the truth, that He is the only way to the Father.

Since the days when Jesus walked in the Holy Land, faithful Christians have found peace in knowing the full promises of God. They could face death, and even joke with their executioners, because they saw their reward. And that reward was not earned, it was a gift for the sake of the death and resurrection of Jesus Christ, our Lord.

"Blessed are you when others revile you and persecute you and utter all kinds of evil against you falsely on my account. Rejoice and be glad, for your reward is great in heaven, for so they persecuted the prophets who were before you." Amen

10/12/2020 – *Law and Gospel* – Romans 8:3–4

Romans 8:3–4

> 3 For God has done what the law, weakened by the flesh, could not do. By sending his own Son in the likeness of sinful flesh and for sin, he condemned sin in the flesh,
>
> 4 in order that the righteous requirement of the law might be fulfilled in us, who walk not according to the flesh but according to the Spirit. (ESV)

You will hear many people suggest that the Bible is filled with contradictions. On one hand, God is a god of vengeance, punishing sinners temporally and eternally. On the other hand, God is a god of grace, offering love and eternal life to each person through His Son, Jesus Christ.

Many of the seeming contradictions can be easily understood if we realize the Bible has two great doctrines, the teaching of the Law and the teaching of the Gospel. Saint Paul explained: "For God has done what the law, weakened by the flesh, could not do. By sending his own Son in the likeness of sinful flesh and for sin, he condemned sin in the flesh, in order that the righteous requirement of the law might be fulfilled in us, who walk not according to the flesh but according to the Spirit."

In effect, Paul explains the purpose of both teachings. The Law condemns each sinner, and shows that we are all sinners. The Gospel shows us Jesus Christ, that we are redeemed from sin and death by His crucifixion and resurrection.

Over the next few weeks we will be looking at the Ten Commandments in light of the two great teachings in the Bible, namely Law and Gospel. We will learn the purpose of the Law, the meaning of the Law, and see how Christ Jesus fulfilled the Law on our behalf.

May our Lord bless you during this study, that you may better come to know Him, who is our life and our salvation. Amen

10/13/2020 – *The First Use – Part 1* – Luke 10:27

Luke 10:27

> 27 And he answered, "You shall love the Lord your God with all your heart and with all your soul and with all your strength and with all your mind, and your neighbor as yourself." (ESV)

Jesus once asked a lawyer, "What is the law of God?" "And he answered, 'You shall love the Lord your God with all your heart and with all your soul and with all your strength and with all your mind, and your neighbor as yourself.' " This is the perfect summation of God's law, a perfect definition. The law is not about things that we should and should not do, the law is about love.

The first three of the Ten Commandments, as traditionally numbered, speak of our love of God. The last seven speak of our love for each other. Even if we do not know the exact words of every law, if we show love we have fulfilled it.

When we act with selfish motives, we sin against both God and man. At that point, there are eventual consequences. We may not pay those consequences immediately, but some time in the future our selfish acts will come back to haunt us.

The problem comes in, we can never take back those words and actions which harm others. No amount of payment, no actions can un-do the evil we caused, we can only hope to cover the hurt we inflict on others.

Therefore, looking at our actions, looking at our desires, through the eyes of love, we see we have failed. Our only hope to make amends is to have help from someone who is not condemned by the law, who has not sinned against God and man. Our only hope is in Christ Jesus.

When confronted with our sin, when confronted with our selfish nature, we turn to Christ Jesus who is our redemption from sin and death. As we study the law, we must remember God's grace and mercy as shown through the Gospel. May our Lord be with you and bless you this day. Amen

10/14/2020 – *The First Use – Part 2* – 1 Timothy 1:9–10

1 Timothy 1:9–10

> 9 understanding this, that the law is not laid down for the just but for the lawless and disobedient, for the ungodly and sinners, for the unholy and profane, for those who strike their fathers and mothers, for murderers,
>
> 10 the sexually immoral, men who practice homosexuality, enslavers, liars, perjurers, and whatever else is contrary to sound doctrine, (ESV)

The summary of God's law is love, that being our love towards God and our love for our neighbor. As we look at how God's law is used, we also see His loving and gracious hand. Many times the law is compared to a curb, a mirror, and a guideline.

Saint Paul, writing to Timothy, said: "...the law is not laid down for the just but for the lawless and disobedient, for the ungodly and sinners, for the unholy and profane, for those who strike their fathers and mothers, for murderers, the sexually immoral, men who practice homosexuality, enslavers, liars, perjurers, and whatever else is contrary to sound doctrine,"

The first use of the law is that of a curb. We know that everyone has sinned, we are conceived and born sinful. It is part of our genetic makeup, passed from father to child.

In love, God desires that we not hurt either our neighbors or ourselves. Thus He is clear that there is a severe penalty for breaking His law. That penalty is death.

As we continue discussing God's law, as we look at the Ten Commandments, we will see that our heavenly Father has a plan to rescue us from sin and death. That plan does not depend on our ability to keep the law perfectly. That plan is the reason Jesus Christ was born, crucified, and rose again.

May our Lord be with you this day. Amen.

10/15/2020 – *The Second Use – Part 1* – 1 John 1:10

1 John 1:10

> 10 If we say we have not sinned, we make him a liar, and his word is not in us. (ESV)

In many respects, the health-care system and the church are similar. Both are concerned with your well being, that you live a long, productive, and healthy life. Thus the health-care professionals urge you to get annual checkups, to be tested if you believe you have been exposed to the COVID 19 virus, to have a colonoscopy after you turn fifty, and to live a healthy lifestyle. They are helping you to live longer than the average person.

The church wants you to live forever. God's law, like the cancer screening done at the doctor's office, shows that there is a problem. That problem is sin.

The law acts as a mirror. When we examine ourselves in the mirror of the law, we know that we have fallen short of God's desires. Saint John, the Evangelist, wrote: "If we say we have not sinned, we make him a liar, and his word is not in us." And like that diagnosis of cancer, we know that we must deal with the problem immediately.

Only as we know of the disease of sin do we realize we must turn to the one cure, Jesus Christ. The mirror of the law prepares you to hear that the Gospel is for you, that Christ has paid the price of your sin. The mirror of the law shows us God's love, that He desires us to know of our diseased condition so we may be treated.

May our Lord bless you this day, as you truly know His love and mercy. Amen.

10/16/2020 – *The Second Use – Part 2* – 1 John 1:10

1 John 1:10

> 10 If we say we have not sinned, we make him a liar, and his word is not in us. (ESV)

God's law always accuses us of our sin. We know that He does not compare our sins to others, but to His divine perfection. Since the fall of Adam, every person conceived in the natural way is conceived and born with sin. We sin because we are sinners, from the moment we began to exist.

People immediately deny this. Time and again we hear them say, "I am not as bad as a Hitler or a Stalin or..." and we insert our favorite name. But one flaw is enough to condemn, one sin is enough to give us eternal death. That is why John the Evangelist wrote: "If we say we have not sinned, we make him a liar, and his word is not in us."

When the mirror of the law does its work, when the mirror of the law shows us the truth, then we are prepared to hear the good news that Jesus Christ died and rose again that you may be declared holy in God's sight. That good news, the Gospel, changes everything. Though we are, while walking this earth, completely a sinner, in God's sight, for the sake of Jesus Christ, we are, even now, completely a saint.

May our Lord bless you this day, as you contemplate His grace and mercy. Amen.

10/19/2020 – *The Third Use* – Proverbs 6:23

Proverbs 6:23

> 23 For the commandment is a lamp and the teaching a light, and the reproofs of discipline are the way of life. (ESV)

For those who are redeemed by God's rich grace and favor for the sake of Jesus Christ, the law presents a different face. Although, as sinners, we still need both the curb and mirror of the law, as saints we see the law as a guideline, something we desire to accomplish out of our love for God. The Proverb of Solomon reminds us: "For the commandment is a lamp and the teaching a light, and the reproofs of discipline are the way of life."

Knowing that love is the fulfillment of the law, we seek to love both God and our neighbor. Our desire is to serve God by reflecting His love and grace to those around us. We look at the law, only to say, "that is what I want to do." And, because we are declared holy and righteous in God's sight, that is what we accomplish.

Those who reject God's mercy cannot use the law as a guideline. The prophet Isaiah wrote, "We have all become like one who is unclean, and all our righteous deeds are like a polluted garment."[44] Isaiah 64:6 Everything they do is tainted by their sin.

What is even more amazing, according to Jesus, those who have been saved by God's undeserved love are frequently unaware of doing good for their neighbors. Good works, following the guidelines of the law, become second nature, done without thinking, simply because Christians reflect God's love. What a pleasant thought.

May our Lord bless you this day, as you go about your daily tasks. Amen.

---

[44] Isaiah 64:6a (ESV)

10/03/2020 – *No Other Gods – Part 1* – Exodus 20:3

Exodus 20:3

> 3 You shall have no other gods before me. (ESV)

God has given us the ten commandments, not to make our lives difficult, but to help us live in happiness and peace. Each of the commandments is given to help us in our relationship with God or with others.

"You shall have no other gods before me." We know that this law serves three purposes, that of a curb, a mirror, and a guideline.

As a curb, we find that all false gods, all idols, be it money, possessions, fame, or even the rocks from the earth, demand that we do something to earn our standing. It is hard work, physically, mentally, and emotionally, to become rich, to own the goodies and toys that define success. Fame brings stress and hardship, causing divorce and even suicide.

Only the true God worshiped by Christians demands nothing. He first comes to us, invites us into His presence, and has redeemed us through the death and resurrection of Jesus Christ. Life everlasting is a gift, it is not earned.

Who would not want to serve such a God? We love Him because He first loved us and sent His Son to free us from the bonds of sin. Our hope is not in the hard, stressful work we do, but in His love.

We have a paradox. The first commandment, the first law of God, is truly an invitation to serve our creator rather than creation. We will see that serving Him becomes natural, an outgrowth of His love for us.

May God grant you His grace this day as we serve Him by serving each other. Amen.

10/21/2020 – *No Other Gods* – Part 2 – Exodus 20:3

Exodus 20:3

> 3 You shall have no other gods before me. (ESV)

The first commandment, "You shall have no other gods before me," is an invitation to love and trust our Creator above all other things. The mirror of the law, however, shows that we have failed in this endeavor. We have loved things before loving the one true God.

That which is important we do. On a Sunday morning, when God invites us into His presence to receive life and salvation, we often ignore that invitation. Sports, sleep, and hobbies become our god. Football cannot give you eternal life. Sleeping late on Sunday will not relieve your concerns about failing to properly serve others. Hobbies do not give the hope which comes from knowing your sins are forgiven.

As the mirror of the law works to convict us of our sin, even the sin of idolatry, we are given the grace of God. In His love, He sent Jesus Christ, the second person of the Trinity, to live perfectly under the law on our behalf. True God and true man, Jesus paid the price of our transgressions. He, and only He, was able to fear, love, and trust in God above all things.

The first commandment certainly is about love, God's love for us, and that we desire to serve Him.

May God give you peace that you know His love and mercy. Amen.

10/22/2020 – *No Other Gods – Part 3* – Exodus 20:3

Exodus 20:3

> 3 You shall have no other gods before me. (ESV)

Adam's sin, that which is passed from father to child, that which we call original sin, is the selfishness that demands that the world conforms to our desires. Adam and Eve gave in to the temptation to be like God, to replace God. Now, as each person looks for their own benefit, we have conflict, hatred, and stress.

God said, through Moses, "You shall have no other gods before me." This takes our eyes off of our own selfishness, our own temptation to be god, and places it on another. As we learn that God is love, that His desire is for all people to be saved and come to the knowledge of the truth, we see that we do not have the ability to replace Him. We are His creation and will, in the end, see we are powerless.

But God, in His mercy, has sent His Son, Jesus, to redeem us from even this selfish nature. Our eyes are on Jesus, the author and perfecter of our faith. We therefore see others through the eyes of Jesus.

As a guideline or rule, this commandment gives us the blessing of knowing that God is in charge. Because we have received God's love, we reflect that love to others. Our selfish desires disappear as we seek to serve our neighbors as God has served us. Our lives are easier because we do not give in to the conflict caused by selfishness.

May our Lord bless you as He uses your hands to show His love to those around you. Amen.

10/23/2020 – *Graven Images* – Exodus 20:4–6

Exodus 20:4–6

> 4 You shall not make for yourself a carved image, or any likeness of anything that is in heaven above, or that is in the earth beneath, or that is in the water under the earth.
>
> 5 You shall not bow down to them or serve them, for I the LORD your God am a jealous God, visiting the iniquity of the fathers on the children to the third and the fourth generation of those who hate me,
>
> 6 but showing steadfast love to thousands of those who love me and keep my commandments. (ESV)

Many Protestant church bodies have a slightly different listing of the Ten Commandments. Lutherans, Roman Catholics, and the Jewish numbering consider these verses as God's commentary on the idols of this world. Others count these verses as the Second Commandment. "You shall not make for yourself a carved image, or any likeness of anything that is in heaven above, or that is in the earth beneath, or that is in the water under the earth. You shall not bow down to them or serve them, for I the LORD your God am a jealous God, visiting the iniquity of the fathers on the children to the third and the fourth generation of those who hate me, but showing steadfast love to thousands of those who love me and keep my commandments."

From the very day that Moses descended from Mount Sinai with the original two tables of stone, the children of Israel showed a problem with worshiping an unseen God. They wanted something to represent Him, thus the golden calf.

We may not carve a golden calf, but we certainly do have our idols, those things other than God in which we place our trust. These verses expose our desire to worship things, to make an idol out of the works of our own hands. These verses show our selfish nature.

As we look to Christ Jesus as our savior from sin and death, we realize that things are just things. Throughout history the faithful people of God have shown reverence by depicting the stories of God's love through art, science, and music. They have not worshiped the art, science, and music, however.

May God keep your heart and mind on His love even as we give Him thanks for the talents of artists and musicians who show us the beauty of His creation. Amen.

10/26/2020 – *Name of God – Part 1* – Exodus 20:7

Exodus 20:7

> 7 You shall not take the name of the LORD your God in vain, for the LORD will not hold him guiltless who takes his name in vain. (ESV)

To know someone's name is to have some power over them. Because of our selfish nature, however, we do not easily remember the names of those we meet, thereby showing them that they are not important. We name our children, we give nick-names to those we love, thus showing they have a special place in our hearts.

God said, through Moses: "You shall not take the name of the LORD your God in vain, for the LORD will not hold him guiltless who takes his name in vain." He desires that we use His name properly, to call upon Him in any trouble, to pray, to praise, to give thanks. This is a true blessing, for by properly using God's name, we acknowledge His great love for us.

Because we have been redeemed from sin and death by Jesus Christ, because we have been brought into God's family through baptism, we desire to know more about Him. God's name reveals who He is, the everlasting Creator, the one who is called "I AM."

By properly using His name, we are assured that He hears our prayers, that He, in turn, calls us by name. The children's hymn, "I Am Jesus' Little Lamb," reminds us that God properly uses our name. He knows us and says, "Your sins, my dear child, are forgiven."

God grant you the peace which comes from knowing and properly using His name. Amen.

10/27/2020 – *Name of God – Part 2* – Exodus 20:7

Exodus 20:7

> 7 You shall not take the name of the LORD your God in vain, for the LORD will not hold him guiltless who takes his name in vain. (ESV)

God's name is special, it shows His creative power, His grace, and His mercy. Jesus' name tells us, "the LORD is our salvation." No wonder the angel told Joseph in a dream what to name the child which Mary bore.

Because we know the strong nature of God's name, even those who have no desire to know of Him misuse His name. For them, the name Jesus Christ is invoked only when an errant hammer blow hits their thumb. For them, the name of God is invoked to condemn a person or object to the depths of hell.

That is actively misusing God's name. Where we properly call upon Him by name in our prayers, in worship, in thanksgiving, others use His name as a magical incantation. They speak His name to lie, to cheat, and to defraud others.

We pray, therefore, that all the names by which God is known may be used with reverence and respect, both to His glory and to our blessing.

May our Lord be with you this day in all things as you call upon Him. Amen.

10/28/2020 – *Name of God – Part 3* – Exodus 20:7

Exodus 20:7

> 7 You shall not take the name of the LORD your God in vain, for the LORD will not hold him guiltless who takes his name in vain. (ESV)

God told Moses: "You shall not take the name of the LORD your God in vain, for the LORD will not hold him guiltless who takes his name in vain." For many people, this means never speaking the name of God. In our English Bibles, God's name is either translated as Jehovah or rendered in all-capital letters. The sacred four letters are hidden, even as they are not spoken in the Synagogues.

There is a proper way to use God's name, especially in prayer. We misuse His name when we pray in such a way where those listening are unsure to whom we are speaking. Often we will hear prayers addressed to "Almighty God," and end, "in Your name we pray." But they do not mention the name of God. Because believers in both the Triune God and idols believe that their god is almighty, this is a way to sound spiritual but make no commitment.

There is the fear that some in the audience will be offended if we pray in the name of Jesus or in a way which identifies us as Christian. They are not the one being addressed. They may show their agreement with the prayer by saying, "amen," or they can remain silent.

As Christians, we boldly proclaim the name of Him Who Died to redeem us from sin and death, Jesus Christ. When we pray, we call upon our Father in heaven because of His Son, as we are given faith by the working of the Holy Spirit. We properly use God's name in private and public prayer, knowing that silence is, at times, not a virtue.

May our Lord grant you peace as you call upon Him this day. Amen.

10/29/2020 – *Sabbath Day – Part 1* – Exodus 20:8

Exodus 20:8

> 8 Remember the Sabbath day to keep it holy. (ESV)

According to legend, the proverb "All work and no play makes Jack a dull boy," was first published in 1659. God, in His love, commanded that we take at least one day off out of every seven. Working without a break, without time off, is unhealthy both physically and mentally.

God said, through Moses, "Remember the Sabbath day to keep it holy." For some people, this means hyper-vigilance to keep from doing any work. For others, it means going to church, or the equivalent in their belief system. The rest of the day is for enjoying in any way they desire.

The Sabbath rest is a time for reflecting on God's love, grace, and mercy. Our Lord cares for our spiritual needs, hence the forgiveness of sins for the sake of the innocent suffering and death of Jesus Christ. Our Lord cares for our physical needs, both as Jesus directed us to pray for our daily bread and that God desires we step away from our daily toils.

How we spend this Sabbath is important. Often we ignore the command to rest, putting in long hours of labor for some tangible or intangible reward. That eventually takes a physical and mental toll.

As Christians, we desire to remember the Sabbath by joining together at God's invitation to receive from Him the good gifts of salvation, forgiveness, and the peace which passes all understanding. There is no better way to keep the letter and spirit of this commandment.

May our Lord bless you with the opportunity to take time to study His Word, to receive the blessings of the Sabbath rest. Amen.

10/30/2020 – *Sabbath Day – Part 2* – Exodus 20:8

Exodus 20:8

8   Remember the Sabbath day to keep it holy. (ESV)

Martin Luther explained the commandment, "Remember the Sabbath day to keep it holy." He wrote, "We should fear and love God so that we do not despise preaching and His Word, but hold it sacred and gladly hear and learn it."

Within a few years of Jesus' resurrection, many Christians began meeting on Sunday rather than Saturday so to celebrate a "little Easter" each week. Because the ceremonial law was fulfilled by Jesus, Christians were free to change their day of rest. This is mentioned several times in the book of Acts.

Changing the day upon which we gather does not change the blessing which comes from hearing the Word of God. Our Lord invites us into His presence so to bestow upon us the good gifts of forgiveness, salvation, eternal life, and the true peace which comes from knowing we are reconciled to God.

Gathering on Sunday morning is not our work to please God, which makes such a gathering into a law we must follow, but God's work to give to us His grace. Certainly we get to respond to His love with our songs of praise and adoration, but the true rhythm of the Divine Service is from God to us, then we speak in thanksgiving.

Thus it is a privilege to set aside one day a week to come into God's presence. He serves us, He applies the benefits of Jesus' death and resurrection to us. There is no greater blessing, no greater gift of love.

"Remember the Sabbath day to keep it holy." Amen.

11/02/2020 – *Sabbath Day – Part 3* – Exodus 20:8

Exodus 20:8

8 Remember the Sabbath day to keep it holy. (ESV)

Early in Jesus' ministry, He and his disciples were walking through a grain field. They were hungry, so they plucked a few heads of grain and began to eat. The Pharisees were indignant. Jesus told the Pharisees, "The Sabbath was made for man, not man for the Sabbath."

Many Sabbath day rituals cause more distress than rest. A rabbi once explained the modifications his family had to make to their stove and refrigerator to ensure they did not inadvertently break the Sabbath laws. The same rules impacted his ability to work weekend shifts to support the health care facility in which he worked.

Such rules and laws put more emphasis on our actions and take our eyes off the reason for the Sabbath. God wants us to be spiritually and physically refreshed. He wants us to receive His gifts of grace, to have time to ponder His Word, and to rejuvenate before we resume our daily tasks. This commandment shows us God's love.

"Remember the Sabbath day to keep it holy." Amen.

11/03/2020 – *Sabbath Day – Part 4* – Exodus 20:8

Exodus 20:8

8 Remember the Sabbath day to keep it holy. (ESV)

By the traditional reckoning of the Ten Commandments, the first three discuss our relationship with God, the last seven discuss our relationship with our neighbor. Martin Luther, in the *Large Catechism,* summarized the first three commandments.

Let me tell you this, even though you know God's Word perfectly and are already a master in all things: you are daily in the devil's kingdom. He ceases neither day nor night to sneak up on you and to kindle in your heart unbelief and wicked thoughts against these [first] three commandments and all the commandments. Therefore you must always have God's Word in your heart, upon your lips, and in your ears. But where the heart is idle and the Word does not make a sound, the devil breaks in and has done the damage before we are aware. On the other hand, the Word is so effective that whenever it is seriously contemplated, heard, and used, it is bound never to be without fruit. It always awakens new understanding, pleasure, and devoutness and produces a pure heart and pure thoughts. For these words are not lazy or dead, but are creative, living words. And even though no other interest or necessity moves us, this truth ought to urge everyone to the Word, because thereby the devil is put to flight and driven away. Besides, this commandment is fulfilled and this exercise in the Word is more pleasing to God than any work of hypocrisy, however brilliant.[45]

May our Lord's Word bring you comfort and joy this day. Amen.

---

[45] Large Catechism I 100-102

11/04/2020 – *Honor – Part 1* – Exodus 20:12

Exodus 20:12

> 12 Honor your father and your mother, that your days may be long in the land that the LORD your God is giving you. (ESV)

The Ten Commandments are an exercise in practical theology. Where other aspects of the church, such as translating of the Bible into modern languages, the study of doctrine, the ceremony surrounding the services in God's house, may be more appealing, how we relate to God and neighbor is of the utmost importance.

Thus God, in His infinite grace, wisdom, love, and mercy, gave us guidelines which will help us deal with one another. We have already seen how we respond to God, by trusting in Him, calling upon Him, and studying His holy Word. Now we learn how to deal with each other, how to make sure that our own selfish desires do not impact our relationships with friends, family, and neighbor.

God told Moses: "Honor your father and your mother, that your days may be long in the land that the LORD your God is giving you." From this Commandment flows all the relationships between family members and society. In the next few days we will see how we honor and respect all in authority, and how that authority comes from the parental office.

There is a lot more to this commandment than simply children honoring parents. This is the first and only commandment with an explicit blessing.

May our Lord richly bless you this day as you serve your neighbor by showing respect and honor. Amen.

11/05/2020 – *Honor – Part 2* – Exodus 20:12

Exodus 20:12

> 12 Honor your father and your mother, that your days may be long in the land that the LORD your God is giving you. (ESV)

God told Moses: "Honor your father and your mother, that your days may be long in the land that the LORD your God is giving you." What does this mean in a practical sense?

God has given a special distinction to fatherhood and motherhood. We are not only supposed to love our parents, but also to honor and respect them. Certainly we are to show love to our siblings, to our neighbors, and to all those with whom we interact. But we show greater respect to our parents.

It is a greater thing to honor than to love. Honor includes not only love, but also deference, humility, and modesty. Honor not only demands we address our parents affectionately and reverently, but that our actions show we respect them very highly. Indeed, parents stand next to God, Himself, in deserving our honor and respect.

Even if we might be embarrassed by our parents, and what child has not been shamed by the "dad jokes" or revealing of family customs, we are to honor our parents. The parental office, given by God for the good of the family, and by extension, the good of society, is the most important office anyone can hold.

May our Lord bless you this day as you give thanks to Him for the blessing of the family into which you were born or adopted. Amen.

11/06/2020 – *Honor – Part 3* – Exodus 20:12

Exodus 20:12

> 12 Honor your father and your mother, that your days may be long in the land that the LORD your God is giving you. (ESV)

Being a parent is hard work. To do it well you need the patience of Job, the wisdom of Solomon, and the love of God, the Father, Himself. No one can be the perfect parent. Yet God says, "Honor your father and your mother."

Raising pious, respectful children begins with the parent's commitment to the first three commandments. With God in the center of the family, there is a much higher probability of success. Though we are aware that no perfect human exists, we do know that as we reflect God's love, grace, and mercy, we are much more successful in our interpersonal relationships.

Being a family member means we need to know of God's forgiveness. More than our neighbors, more than our friends, our families need to practice mutual respect and tolerance. After all, who is closer than parents to their children?

There is no magic bullet, just acknowledging our sin to each other, and giving forgiveness when others sin against us. After all, our heavenly Father has forgiven all of our sins for the sake of Christ Jesus. We can do likewise as we have faith in Christ Jesus.

As parents, we need to be worthy of the honor given by our children. We need to look first to God and then reflect His love to those who are most precious.

May our Lord richly bless you this day as you serve your family with love. Amen.

11/09/2020 – *Honor – Part 4* – Exodus 20:12

Exodus 20:12

> 12 Honor your father and your mother, that your days may be long in the land that the LORD your God is giving you. (ESV)

God directed Moses to record, "Honor your father and your mother, that your days may be long in the land that the LORD your God is giving you." This is the first and only commandment with a direct promise.

All authority derives from the authority of parents. The family is the bedrock of society. If families are strong, society is also strong. As families grow weaker, as men refuse to take responsibility for children, as women terminate their pregnancies, as divorce rates rise, society suffers. Compare the American society of the late eighteenth century to society today. We are worse off than our grandparents and great-grandparents.

Honoring authority takes personal responsibility. It also takes a willingness to defer to someone else for the good of everyone. This goes against the grain, it is not in our nature to think of others before ourselves.

Yet God, in His love, has given us the model, both of fatherhood and of respect. Jesus Christ loved and respected His Father so much, He obeyed His Father's will that caused Him to bear the burden of our sin.

May our Lord richly bless you and your family as you respond to His love by giving honor and respect to others. Amen.

11/10/2020 – *Honor – Part 5* – Exodus 20:12

Exodus 20:12

> 12 Honor your father and your mother, that your days may be long in the land that the LORD your God is giving you. (ESV)

We have been studying the fourth commandment, "Honor your father and your mother, that your days may be long in the land that the LORD your God is giving you."

Martin Luther summarized the duties of parents and children in the "Table of Duties" in his "Small Catechism." He wrote:

> For Parents: Ye fathers, provoke not your children to wrath, but bring them up in the nurture and admonition of the Lord. Eph. 6:4.
>
> For Children: Children, obey your parents in the Lord; for this is right. Honor thy father and mother; which is the first commandment with promise: that it may be well with thee, and thou mayest live long on the earth. Eph. 6:1-3.

And to all citizens, Luther counseled:

> Let every soul be subject unto the higher powers. For the power which exists anywhere is ordained of God. Whosoever resisteth the power resisteth the ordinance of God; and they that resist shall receive to themselves damnation. For he beareth not the sword in vain; for he is the minister of God, a revenger to execute wrath upon him that doeth evil. Rom. 13:1-4.

May God grant that each of us hear His Word, that we respect each other, and that we receive the blessings He gives as we live according to His commandments. Amen.

11/11/2020 – *Murder – Part 1* – Exodus 20:13

Exodus 20:13

13 You shall not murder. (ESV)

Having dealt with both parental and civil authority, which are given as God's gift to each individual, we now turn our attention to our neighbor. God told Moses, "You shall not murder."

One of the first questions we must ask, does this commandment apply to the civil government in cases where a criminal, one who disrespects the laws of the land to the harm of others, is given the death penalty? No, for Saint Paul reminds us that the civil authorities wield the sword, literally the power of life and death, for the good of society.

In the case of parents, they also are allowed to discipline their children, though they should not cause physical harm. Again, the undisciplined child not only disrupts the family, but society in general.

As an individual, we have no right to harm another, to take their life or to inflict injury. We must not kill, either by our actions, by our hatred, or by our words. Our intent is to befriend and care for our neighbors, especially the ones who cause us the most grief.

May God grant us the will and strength of character to love our neighbor as our heavenly Father has loved us, to our blessing and the benefit of all. Amen.

11/12/2020 – *Murder – Part 2* – Exodus 20:13

Exodus 20:13

13 You shall not murder. (ESV)

God told Moses, "You shall not murder." Jesus told His disciples: "You have heard that it was said to those of old, 'You shall not murder; and whoever murders will be liable to judgment.' But I say to you that everyone who is angry with his brother will be liable to judgment; whoever insults his brother will be liable to the council; and whoever says, 'You fool!' will be liable to the hell of fire."[46] Matthew 5:21–22

Murder, therefore, is not only harming another, but bearing any ill will. It also means we may be guilty of offending against this commandment by our inaction as well as actions. If we see our neighbor in need and do nothing, we have sinned against them. Martin Luther reminded his hearers:

> If you send a person away naked when you could clothe him, you have let him freeze to death. If you see anyone suffer hunger and do not feed him, you have let him starve.[47]

As we look at the Commandments, as we ponder the First Commandment, we see that God desires to help us in every need, to shower us with His love, to cause us to be saved from sin and death. Is not helping our neighbor, is not caring them physically, simply reflecting the love that our heavenly Father first gave us? His love is for all people, and we reflect that love to everyone we meet.

May our Lord bless you richly as you reflect God's love in all that you do. Amen.

---

[46] Matthew 5:21-22 (ESV)
[47] Large Catechism, Fifth Commandment

11/13/2020 – *Adultery – Part 1* – Exodus 20:14

Exodus 20:14

13 You shall not commit adultery. (ESV)

The Ten Commandments flow in a logical order. First you have the three commandments which define our relationship to God. Then we speak of authority, which derives from parenthood and flows through all society. We protect our neighbor's life. We protect our neighbor's marriage.

At the risk of being politically incorrect, marriage is defined as the joining of a male and female. Although God allowed polygamy, marriage in the best sense is the life-long union of a husband and wife.

There are three Biblical reasons for marriage. The first is procreation, having and raising children. The second is for companionship, for God observed of Adam, "It is not good that the man should be alone; I will make him a helper fit for him."[48] Genesis 2:18 The third is to curb sinful lust.

In the great passage about marriage in the book of Ephesians, Paul suggests that marriage involves mutual submission, the husband loving the wife and deferring to her, while the wife honors the husband. Both seek the best for the other. Marriage is about your spouse, not yourself.

Having noted what the Bible says about marriage, may our Lord bless you as you live within your family, loving your spouse as Christ Jesus loves His bride, the church. Amen.

---

[48] Genesis 2:18 (ESV)

11/16/2020 – *Adultery – Part 2* – Exodus 20:14

Exodus 20:14

13 You shall not commit adultery. (ESV)

God told Moses, "You shall not commit adultery." God created male and female for their mutual blessing. Any actions which are reserved for husband and wife which happen outside the context of marriage weaken the bonds which hold the family together.

It is God's desire that, unless married, we refrain from intimate relations. Such restraint brings many blessings, a freedom from concern about pregnancy, a deepened respect for each other, a stronger family. It is also God's desire that, once a husband and wife are joined in marriage, that they stay married. The promise, "Until we are parted by death," should not be taken lightly. No one, not the parents, not the children, not the relatives, are blessed when a marriage fails.

As we have earlier learned, the strong family is the foundation of a strong society. God gave us this commandment so that we strive to love, honor, respect, and serve our spouse for the good of everyone.

May you enjoy the blessing which God has given when He placed you into your family. Amen.

11/17/2020 – *Property* – *Part 1* – Exodus 20:15

Exodus 20:15

> 13 You shall not steal. (ESV)

Next to our lives and our families, our biggest concern is property. Thus the order of the commandments, "You shall not murder," "You shall not commit adultery," and "You shall not steal."

Immediately, as we hear "You shall not steal," we may think of theft or looting. One of the justifications we heard from those looting stores during the riots this summer, "The stores have insurance to cover these losses." Someone is paying for the large-format flat-screen television the looter is stealing in compensation for a perceived wrong perpetuated decades or centuries ago. As a society, we cannot condone such thinking. It hurts our neighbors, it hurts those who are trying to serve us.

Armed robbery falls into the same category. We are, as a society, against anyone who demands, with the threat of violence, that which is not theirs.

Certainly this commandment, "You shall not steal," protects us from those who by violent means, by breaking and entering, by extortion, would take that for which they have not labored. In this we are all in agreement.

In the next few days we are going to look at other implications of this commandment, ones that may hit a bit closer to home. In the meanwhile, may our Lord bless you as you enjoy the rich gifts He has given to you. Amen.

11/18/2020 – *Property* – Part 2 – Exodus 20:15

Exodus 20:15

> 13 You shall not steal. (ESV)

God directed Moses to write, "You shall not steal." Certainly, most of us have never overtly stolen from another. We respect the time and effort needed to earn the money to purchase those items we want or need.

Then again, what about vandalism? We watched in horror as mobs attacked the Empire Mall in Sioux Falls last summer. We were abhorred as we saw the fires in Minneapolis as people protested the death of George Floyd. We were aghast that even Kenosha, Wisconsin, the home of the Rambler automobile, erupted with violence and death.

These actions by the out-of-control mobs were harming innocent people, the merchants who watched their stores being destroyed, the employees who lost their jobs as companies were forced to close. To what good was that vandalism? Who did it serve? Did it resurrect Mister Floyd? Did it bring new respect for social minorities?

The crimes against property are stealing. They take away our livelihood, our ability to care for our families. They harm both our neighbors and ourselves.

"You shall not steal" is God's call for us to love our neighbors, to care for them, to use our property for the good of all. This is not a zero-sum game where your gain is my loss, but a way of enhancing each of our lives. It is an opportunity to show our respect for each other, to improve your life while improving mine.

May our Lord grant us wisdom to properly use and care for both our own property and the property of others. Amen.

11/19/2020 – *Property – Part 3* – Exodus 20:15

Exodus 20:15

13 You shall not steal. (ESV)

"You shall not steal," God said through Moses. Let's look at some of the ways we might be stealing. The cover of the October 3, 1936 edition of the *Saturday Evening Post* shows a whimsical picture of a grocer weighing a chicken while the customer, a prim and proper older woman, looks on. The grocer has his finger on the scale, while the matron is lifting the scale with her right hand. Both are stealing.

Those who sell goods or services have the obligation to give the best return for their customer's money. Providing shoddy merchandise or bad service is stealing from the very people who are allowing you to remain in business. The surly waiter, the disinterested clerk, does a disservice to their employer, for they drive away customers.

Thus, in keeping this commandment, those who sell have an obligation to give good value. This is as simple as properly representing the goods and services offered. This is as simple as saying a heart-felt "thank you" to those you serve. This is as simple as being available as needed, especially in times of emergencies.

"A false balance is an abomination to the LORD, but a just weight is his delight,"[49] Proverbs 11:1 Solomon wrote. May this guide our relationships to those we serve.

God grant you His rich blessings this day as you are privileged to serve your neighbor. Amen.

---

[49] Proverbs 11:1 (ESV)

11/20/2020 – *Property – Part 4* – Exodus 20:15

Exodus 20:15

> 13 You shall not steal. (ESV)

As we look at the commandment "You shall not steal," we realize that we have a responsibility towards all people. Just as we expect merchants and service-providers to be honest in their dealings, we have a responsibility as customers.

How do we act when we are shopping? A manager at an automobile dealership in Colorado suggested that most customers are not truthful. He also claimed that they would try to kill the salesman during the test drive. Time and again the customer was seen as being overbearing, demanding, and unreasonable. The customer may simply have been reacting to the high-pressure sales tactics at that particular dealership.

As a customer, we need to take care not to harm the merchandise as we examine it. Although we may reject an item, someone else may select it. If, however, we damage the goods, we have stolen from the merchant.

Even as customers, we look to serve our neighbor. It is our goal to reflect God's love to everyone, thus our actions are truly important.

May our Lord continue to bless and keep you as you reflect His grace and love. Amen.

11/23/2020 – *Property* – *Part 5* – Exodus 20:15

Exodus 20:15

> 13 You shall not steal. (ESV)

We have been dealing with the commandment, "You shall not steal," from the viewpoint of crimes, of respect for property, as service providers, and as customers. There is one other area where we may be stealing, that of employment.

Employers owe their employees a wage commensurate with the responsibilities of the job. Some jobs are not meant to support a family, but are a part-time experience to gain knowledge and skills. The paper routes we had in junior high, working as a dishwasher while in high school, gave us a glimpse into the world of business. We learned to provide good service with a smile. For this we got paid, not a princely sum, but enough to provide for some savings and the occasional Friday night date.

As employees, we need to give a full day's work for our agreed-upon wages. We cannot slack off, be surly to the customers, or do shoddy work. Our responsibility is to be an asset to our employers, even if we are in an entry-level job.

Stealing is much more than lifting an Amazon package off a front porch, or shoplifting an item from the grocery store. Stealing is doing anything which diminishes the value of another person's property.

May our Lord grant us the wisdom and love to protect our neighbor's possessions, to help them enhance their lives, and in so doing, reflect God's grace and mercy. Amen.

11/24/2020 – *Reputation – Part 1* – Exodus 20:16

Exodus 20:16

16 You shall not bear false witness against your neighbor. (ESV)

So far we have seen that the second tablet of God's law, the Ten Commandments, deals with our relationship to authority, our lives, our families, and our property. God's law also protects our reputation. Moses was given the commandment, "You shall not bear false witness against your neighbor."

Consider the childhood taunt, "Sticks and stones may break my bones, but words will never hurt me." We know that words alone can cause psychological damage, ruin our self-image, and enslave us to misery. Verbal abuse is abuse, and should not be tolerated.

Rumors spread about people certainly can bring them harm. We cease to trust them, we believe the lies or half-truths, we give them no opportunity to explain their actions. Immediately they are accused, judged, condemned, and sentenced with no defense.

This commandment protects our good name in several ways, which we will examine in the coming days. We leave this morning with the thought that God loves us so much that He gives us life, family, property, and reputation. He loves us so much that He desires all to be protected, that we may know of His grace and mercy.

May our Lord richly bless you this day. Amen.

11/25/2020 – *Reputation – Part 2* – Exodus 20:16

Exodus 20:16

16 You shall not bear false witness against your neighbor. (ESV)

God gave Moses the commandment, "You shall not bear false witness against your neighbor." In its first and simplest meaning, the words of this commandment pertain to public courts, where we may be asked to testify concerning various situations.

When dealing with those in authority, we tell the truth. We are compelled by this commandment to speak of that which we know, giving the facts but no opinions. If we did not actually see something happen, we cannot speak about it.

Our desire is for justice to always be served. Those who truly disrupt society should be dealt with in a way where they may no longer harm their neighbors. If there is any doubt, however, that the accusations are false, the accused must escape punishment.

Therefore, we are enjoined by this commandment to speak only the truth, only that which we know, and in a way that helps preserve our neighbor's reputation. Nothing is gained by lying to those in authority. In following this commandment, not only do we protect our neighbor, but we also preserve our own reputation.

May our Lord grant you His grace this day. Amen.

11/26/2020 – *Thanksgiving* – 1 Timothy 2:1–4

1 Timothy 2:1–4

> 1 First of all, then, I urge that supplications, prayers, intercessions, and thanksgivings be made for all people,
>
> 2 for kings and all who are in high positions, that we may lead a peaceful and quiet life, godly and dignified in every way.
>
> 3 This is good, and it is pleasing in the sight of God our Savior,
>
> 4 who desires all people to be saved and to come to the knowledge of the truth. (ESV)

Saint Paul wrote to Timothy:

> First of all, then, I urge that supplications, prayers, intercessions, and thanksgivings be made for all people, for kings and all who are in high positions, that we may lead a peaceful and quiet life, godly and dignified in every way. This is good, and it is pleasing in the sight of God our Savior, who desires all people to be saved and to come to the knowledge of the truth.

On this day of Thanksgiving, we pray for our nation and give glory to God for all His blessings.

> Almighty God, You have given us this good land as our heritage. Grant that we remember Your generosity and constantly do Your will. Bless our land with honest industry, truthful education, and an honorable way of life. Save us from violence, discord, and confusion, from pride and arrogance, and from every evil course of action. Make us who came from many nations with many different languages a united people. Defend our liberties, and give those whom we have entrusted with the authority of government, the President and Congress of the United States, the Governor and Legislature of this state, all our judges and magistrates, the spirit of wisdom that there may be justice and

peace in our land. When times are prosperous, let our hearts be thankful; and in troubled times do not let our trust in you fail.

Almighty God, Your mercies are new every morning and You graciously provide for all our needs of body and soul. Grant us Your Holy Spirit that we may acknowledge Your goodness, give thanks for Your benefits and serve You in willing obedience all our days; through Jesus Christ, Your Son, our Lord, who lives and reigns with You and the Holy Spirit, one God, now and forever. Amen.

From Trinity Lutheran Church to you and your family, may our Lord richly bless you this day. Amen.

11/27/2020 – *Reputation – Part 3* – Exodus 20:16

Exodus 20:16

16 You shall not bear false witness against your neighbor. (ESV)

Martin Luther, writing in his "Large Catechism," said this about the commandment, "You shall not bear false witness against your neighbor."

> Next, it extends very much further, if we are to apply it to spiritual jurisdiction or administration; here it is a common occurrence that every one bears false witness against his neighbor. For wherever there are godly preachers and Christians, they must bear the sentence before the world that they are called heretics, apostates, yea, seditious and desperately wicked miscreants. Besides, the Word of God must suffer in the most shameful and malicious manner, being persecuted, blasphemed, contradicted, perverted, and falsely cited and interpreted. But let this pass; for it is the way of the blind world that she condemns and persecutes the truth and the children of God, and yet esteems it no sin.[50]

We see this happening when Christian pastors are asked to pray, but not use the name of Jesus. We see this happening when Christian organizations are slandered for living according to the teachings of the church. We see this happening when congregations seek to destroy the livelihood of their pastors, to force them from the pulpit for being faithful to God's Word.

We pray, therefore, that God's Word, and those who proclaim the truth of His grace, mercy, and love, may be protected from this harm. May our Lord grant you strength this day as you live in His grace. Amen.

---

[50]https://bookofconcord.org/large-catechism/part-i/commandment-viii/

11/30/2020 – *Reputation – Part 4* – Exodus 20:16

Exodus 20:16

16 You shall not bear false witness against your neighbor. (ESV)

The commandment, "You shall not bear false witness against your neighbor," forbids all sins where we may verbally injure or offend our neighbor. Saint James wrote:

> And the tongue is a fire, a world of unrighteousness. The tongue is set among our members, staining the whole body, setting on fire the entire course of life, and set on fire by hell. For every kind of beast and bird, of reptile and sea creature, can be tamed and has been tamed by mankind, but no human being can tame the tongue. It is a restless evil, full of deadly poison.[51] James 3:6–8

We like to spread and hear bad news about people. In so doing, we put on airs, we feel superior, for we would never sin in such a way, we are too intelligent. But, in accepting such gossip, in spreading such gossip, we are causing vicious harm to another's reputation. As Martin Luther wrote, "Evil though we are, we cannot tolerate having evil spoken of us; we want golden compliments of the whole world. Yet, we cannot bear to hear the best spoken of others."[52]

May our Lord grant us the wisdom to reject the gossip of others, and to speak well of our neighbor. Amen.

---

[51] James 3:6-8 (ESV)
[52] Large Catechism, Tappert, p. 400

12/01/2020 – *Reputation – Part 5* – Exodus 20:16

Exodus 20:16

16 You shall not bear false witness against your neighbor. (ESV)

Are there times where the commandment, "You shall not bear false witness against your neighbor," does not apply? Is there a time when we can indeed speak of the evil we have witnessed? In the simplest of terms, when we are called on by the civil authorities to give witness, then, and only then, are we allowed by this commandment to speak of our neighbor's failings.

We must understand this commandment in such a way where evil does not go unpunished. We are obligated, because we seek the best for our neighbors, to protect others from those actions which bring harm.

How do we do this? Jesus told His followers:

> If your brother sins against you, go and tell him his fault, between you and him alone. If he listens to you, you have gained your brother. But if he does not listen, take one or two others along with you, that every charge may be established by the evidence of two or three witnesses. If he refuses to listen to them, tell it to the church. And if he refuses to listen even to the church, let him be to you as a Gentile and a tax collector.[53] Matthew 18:15–17

In civil matters, we follow the same procedure. We deal with the situation privately, then with witnesses, if at all possible. Finally, if appropriate, we speak with the proper authorities.

May our Lord continue to grant us His grace and mercy, that we may properly handle the word of truth to the benefit of our neighbor. Amen.

---

[53] Matthew 18:15-17 (ESV)

12/02/2020 – *Covet – Part 1* – Exodus 20:17

Exodus 20:17

> 17 You shall not covet your neighbor's house; you shall not covet your neighbor's wife, or his male servant, or his female servant, or his ox, or his donkey, or anything that is your neighbor's. (ESV)

Early in Jesus' ministry, Jesus ascended a mountain and taught His disciples. Among the things He said in the Sermon on the Mount:

> You have heard that it was said, You shall not commit adultery. But I say to you that everyone who looks at a woman with lustful intent has already committed adultery with her in his heart.[54] Matthew 5:27–28

In many respects, Jesus was restating the ninth and tenth commandments. "You shall not covet your neighbor's house; you shall not covet your neighbor's wife, or his male servant, or his female servant, or his ox, or his donkey, or anything that is your neighbor's."

Keeping the commandments is not only a matter of our actions, but of our inward desires. To covet is to desire something, to lust after something, that is forbidden to us. Our neighbor's property is our neighbor's. We have no right to it. Our neighbor's wife, his or her employees, his or her livestock, are not available to us.

We will look at other aspects of these two commandments in the next few days. May our Lord make us content with what we have, and give us the wisdom to help our neighbors maintain what is their's. Amen.

---

[54] Matthew 5:27-28 (ESV)

12/03/2020 – *Covet – Part 2* – Exodus 20:17

Exodus 20:17

> 17 You shall not covet your neighbor's house; you shall not covet your neighbor's wife, or his male servant, or his female servant, or his ox, or his donkey, or anything that is your neighbor's. (ESV)

God told Moses, "You shall not covet your neighbor's house; you shall not covet your neighbor's wife, or his male servant, or his female servant, or his ox, or his donkey, or anything that is your neighbor's."

Martin Luther explained these two commandments:

> We should fear and love God that we may not craftily seek to get our neighbor's inheritance or house, and obtain it by a show of justice and right, etc., but help and be of service to him in keeping it.
>
> We should fear and love God that we may not estrange, force, or entice away our neighbor's wife, servants, or cattle, but urge them to stay and diligently do their duty.[55]

Our thoughts and desires precede our actions. If our desires are pure, our actions towards our neighbors will be pure. Thus we pray that our Lord give us the strength and wisdom to properly see the material things of this world as temporary, and grant that we fix our thoughts on those things that last. Even as we are saved from sin and death through faith in Christ Jesus, may we help and defend our neighbor. Amen.

---

[55]Small Catechism – 9th and 10 commandments

12/04/2020 – *Close of the Commandments – Part 1* – Exodus 20:5b–6

Exodus 20:5b–6

> 5b For I the LORD your God am a jealous God, visiting the iniquity of the fathers on the children to the third and the fourth generation of those who hate me,
>
> 6 but showing steadfast love to thousands of those who love me and keep my commandments. (ESV)

For the past few weeks we have been looking at the Ten Commandments. What does God say about these rules for behavior?

> For I the LORD your God am a jealous God, visiting the iniquity of the fathers on the children to the third and the fourth generation of those who hate me, but showing steadfast love to thousands of those who love me and keep my commandments.

It is true that parents teach their children, and the children teach their children. If the parents are faithful towards God, if they seek first His kingdom and righteousness, then the children are likely to also be faithful. If the parents reject God, if they become a law unto themselves, if they act with selfish motives, then the children will do the same.

For many reasons the child of an alcoholic becomes an alcoholic, or the child of a violent parent visits the same violence on their own children. It takes an act of God, literally, the conversion of the heart and will which comes through the working of the Holy Spirit, to break this cycle.

We will look again at the purpose of the Law, of the Ten Commandments, to see how they are a blessing to each person. Today, therefore, may our Lord be with you, granting you His wisdom and peace. Amen.

12/07/2020 – *Close of the Commandments – Part 2* – Romans 13:3–4

Romans 13:3–4

> 3 For rulers are not a terror to good conduct, but to bad. Would you have no fear of the one who is in authority? Then do what is good, and you will receive his approval,
>
> 4 for he is God's servant for your good. But if you do wrong, be afraid, for he does not bear the sword in vain. For he is the servant of God, an avenger who carries out God's wrath on the wrongdoer. (ESV)

We believe, teach, and confess that God gave us the Law, the Ten Commandments, for three purposes. The law acts like a curb, a mirror, and a guideline. Let's look at the purpose of a curb.

Saint Paul wrote:

> For rulers are not a terror to good conduct, but to bad. Would you have no fear of the one who is in authority? Then do what is good, and you will receive his approval, for he is God's servant for your good. But if you do wrong, be afraid, for he does not bear the sword in vain. For he is the servant of God, an avenger who carries out God's wrath on the wrongdoer.

The first use of the law is to cause us to obey because we fear punishment. God has placed civil authorities over us to keep the peace, to enforce the law, to ensure the safety of our lives and property. Those who break the law are punished; those who keep the law live in peace.

There is nothing moral about the first use of the law, it is simply pragmatic. If we do good we have nothing to fear. If we do evil, we pay the price.

God, in His love, desires that we lead quiet and peaceful lives, that we be free from the fear of those in authority. Therefore, He gives us the rules which provide for peace between neighbors.

God grant that we see the wisdom of the first use of the law, that of being a curb, that we may live in harmony with those around us. Amen.

12/08/2020 – *Close of the Commandments – Part 3* – Romans 3:20

Romans 3:20

> 20 For by works of the law no human being will be justified in his sight, since through the law comes knowledge of sin. (ESV)

God's Law was given to us for three reasons. The first was to stop overt bad behavior, to be a curb against sin. The second, today's topic, is to act as a mirror to show us our sin. The third is a guide or rule to tell us how to act.

Saint Paul spoke about the use of the Law as a mirror. "For by works of the law no human being will be justified in his sight, since through the law comes knowledge of sin."

Each of us has failed, each of us has not lived according to God's Law. Knowing that the standard is perfection, we stand condemned. By ourselves we cannot keep the Law, nor can we pay the debt of our past sins. It is the mirror of the Law which drives us to see God's grace and mercy through Jesus Christ.

Jesus fulfilled the Law on our behalf. We do not earn the forgiveness which God gives for the sake of Christ Jesus. It is a gift. When we look in the mirror, we repent and throw ourselves on God's grace.

May our Lord comfort you with His mercy, that the mirror of the Law shows you the depth of His love. Amen.

12/09/2020 – *Close of the Commandments – Part 4* – Psalms 119:105

Psalms 119:105

10 Your word is a lamp to my feet and a light to my path. (ESV)

God gave us His holy Law to curb destructive behaviors, to show us our sin, and to be a guide to act in a proper way towards both God and man. It is the third use of the Law of which the Psalmist says, "Your word is a lamp to my feet and a light to my path." Psalms 119:105

We don't always know the right thing to do. This is why we ask our spouse, "what do you want for our anniversary," or inquire of a friend, "how may I help you." We need the guide, we need to be shown the difference between right and wrong.

Jesus provides the answer,

> And he said to him, You shall love the Lord your God with all your heart and with all your soul and with all your mind. This is the great and first commandment. And a second is like it: You shall love your neighbor as yourself.[56] Matthew 22:37–39

Thus we are to first serve God, to fear, love, and trust in Him above all things. Then we are to love our neighbors, be concerned about them, protect their lives, their families, their property, and their reputation. Love is the summary of all the commandments.

May our Lord grant you the strength and wisdom to love Him above all things, and to love your neighbor as yourself. Amen.

---

[56] Matthew 22:37-39 (ESV)

12/10/2020 – *Close of the Commandments* – *Part 5* – Psalms 119:105

Psalms 119:105

  10 Your word is a lamp to my feet and a light to my path. (ESV)

Of the three uses of God's Law, that of a curb, a mirror, and a guide, the third use is given only to Christians. Our good works, our following the Ten Commandments, our attempts to obey God's Law, will not earn us salvation. The standard is perfection, and each of us has sinned and fall short of the standard.

  We believe, teach, and confess that the forgiveness of sins is a gift from God, given to us for the sake of Christ Jesus. Any attempt to earn our forgiveness by doing good works will, in fact, take the glory from God, thus breaking the First Commandment.

  Christians perform those acts of kindness, those good works which fulfill the commandments, as a response to the forgiveness given to them by God. These good works flow from the love of God which is His gift. We cannot help but reflect His love.

  Therefore, only those who do not look to good works, but look to Christ Jesus, actually are doing good works. All others who rely on themselves are working, not for the good of God and neighbor, but for themselves.

  May our Lord grant you His love, grace, and mercy, that you may truly do everything to His glory. Amen.

12/11/2020 – *The Christmas Story* – Part 1 – Luke 2:1–3

Luke 2:1–3

> 1 In those days a decree went out from Caesar Augustus that all the world should be registered.
>
> 2 This was the first registration when Quirinius was governor of Syria.
>
> 3 And all went to be registered, each to his own town. (ESV)

The first *Peanuts* animated television special aired on December 9, 1965. *A Charlie Brown Christmas* spoke of the problems of the young boy as he dealt with the meaning of the holiday. Near the end of the program, Linus told Charlie Brown the true meaning of Christmas, quoting Saint Luke's account of the birth of Jesus Christ.

So, like Linus and Charlie Brown, we will look at the true meaning of Christmas, the birth of Jesus Christ as our Redeemer from sin and eternal death. In the television special the *Peanuts* gang was producing a Christmas play. In our churches, tradition says we have the children tell the story of the Nativity, causing many to miss the importance of the words as they focus on the cute antics of the Sunday School classes.

We miss that the birth of Jesus Christ was foretold since our first parents turned their backs on God in the days following the Creation. From the first prophecy of a Savior, we know that He was to suffer torture and death so to pay the price of each person's sins. Jesus, the cute baby lying in a manger in the cold stall, was born to die.

Hear the beginning of the account by Saint Luke:

> In those days a decree went out from Caesar Augustus that all the world should be registered. This was the first registration when Quirinius was governor of Syria. And all went to be registered, each to his own town.

May our Lord bless you this day as we ponder the miracle of the Son of God taking upon Himself our humanity so to free us from our sins. Amen.

12/14/2020 – *The Christmas Story – Part 2* – Luke 2:1–3

Luke 2:1–3

> 1 In those days a decree went out from Caesar Augustus that all the world should be registered.
>
> 2 This was the first registration when Quirinius was governor of Syria.
>
> 3 And all went to be registered, each to his own town. (ESV)

>> In those days a decree went out from Caesar Augustus that all the world should be registered. This was the first registration when Quirinius was governor of Syria. And all went to be registered, each to his own town.

Immediately Luke's account of the Nativity of Jesus places Christianity in a unique position among all the world's religions. Christians dare to make the claim that the Son of God was born at a certain time and in a certain place. Luke is clear as to the historical events surrounding the census, giving several references as to the year.

Unlike the religions of Greece and Rome, unlike the pagan or spiritualist beliefs, we can look for hard evidence of the truth of the statements about Jesus' birth. Even after two millenia, records exist which show that Luke was correct in his dates.

Believing the account is a matter of faith, of accepting the story as accurate. All the archaeological proof, all the accounts written in the decades following Jesus' birth, may not convince you that, though the details are correct, Jesus is the Son of God. Yet, time and again archaeologists have discovered that the details are true, in spite of many who would desire to debunk the Bible.

May our Lord comfort you with the fact that Jesus was born at a verifiable time in human history, and walked this earth at a known location. Amen.

12/15/2020 – *The Christmas Story* – Part 3 – Luke 2:4–5

Luke 2:4–5

> 4 And Joseph also went up from Galilee, from the town of Nazareth, to Judea, to the city of David, which is called Bethlehem, because he was of the house and lineage of David,
>
> 5 to be registered with Mary, his betrothed, who was with child. (ESV)

>> And Joseph also went up from Galilee, from the town of Nazareth, to Judea, to the city of David, which is called Bethlehem, because he was of the house and lineage of David, to be registered with Mary, his betrothed, who was with child.

In 1993, archaeologists discovered an ancient fragment of a document which included the words "House of David." Many modern scholars had, up to then, suggested that King David, who plays such an important role in Jewish history, was as mythical as the English King Arthur. Yet, as so often happens, the earth gives up evidence that the Bible is accurate even as it discusses ancient history.

Why is this important? The prophet Isaiah reminds us:

> Of the increase of his government and of peace there will be no end, on the throne of David and over his kingdom, to establish it and to uphold it with justice and with righteousness from this time forth and forevermore. The zeal of the LORD of hosts will do this.[57] Isaiah 9:7

The Savior had to be a descendant of David, which both Matthew and Luke show was the case, both through Joseph and Mary. Christmas, then, is the fulfillment of God's promise to defeat sin, eternal death, and the power of the devil.

May our Lord bless you and your family as we remember God's promise of His grace and love. Amen.

---

[57] Isaiah 9:7 (ESV)

12/16/2020 – *The Christmas Story* – Part 4 – Luke 2:4–5

Luke 2:4–5

> 4 And Joseph also went up from Galilee, from the town of Nazareth, to Judea, to the city of David, which is called Bethlehem, because he was of the house and lineage of David,
>
> 5 to be registered with Mary, his betrothed, who was with child. (ESV)

> And Joseph also went up from Galilee, from the town of Nazareth, to Judea, to the city of David, which is called Bethlehem, because he was of the house and lineage of David, to be registered with Mary, his betrothed, who was with child.

In the first chapter of Saint Luke's Gospel, we are introduced to Mary, the mother of our Lord. She calmly accepted the news that the angel Gabriel brought, that though she was a virgin, she would bear the Son of God. "I am the handmaid of the Lord," she replied. Beyond the great honor of being the mother of the Savior of all people, Mary is a paragon of faith, trusting in God even in the face of a miracle.

Saint Matthew records how Joseph, who had every right to divorce Mary or even have her stoned for being unfaithful, accepted the news that she was carrying Jesus, whose name means "the LORD is our Salvation." He, too, is an example of faith. His actions were crucial to Jesus' survival in the days following the Nativity.

The parents of Jesus were honorable people who trusted God. They gave God the glory by showing honor to the civil authorities, although the journey from Nazareth to Bethlehem was fraught with danger. In faith they set out to the city of David, guided by God for the blessing of all people.

May our Lord bless you and your family the faith to know of God's love, even in difficult circumstances.. Amen.

12/17/2020 – *The Christmas Story* – Part 5 – Luke 2:6–7

Luke 2:6–7

> 6 And while they were there, the time came for her to give birth.
>
> 7 And she gave birth to her firstborn son and wrapped him in swaddling cloths and laid him in a manger, because there was no place for them in the inn. (ESV)

And while they were there, the time came for her to give birth. And she gave birth to her firstborn son and wrapped him in swaddling cloths and laid him in a manger, because there was no place for them in the inn.

No event in history has had the impact of the birth of Jesus, the Messiah. The impact of Jesus touches every aspect of society, from the way we look at marriage and family, to health care, to the morals of leadership, to the way we perform our daily tasks. Even the way we count the days shows the importance of this event.

None of that matters in the long run. The reason that Jesus was born was not to free the slaves, elevate the place of women in society, inaugurate health-care, reform governments, or establish the dignity of all lawful labor. Jesus was born to die for our sins.

The newborn infant, lying in a feed-trough in humble circumstances, is the Son of God through whom all things were made. He is true God and true man, conceived without the sin which clings to our human nature through the working of the Holy Spirit. Though sinless, though not subject to death because of transgressing God's law, Jesus took upon Himself our transgressions. We call this the miracle of the Incarnation, the true wonder of this day.

May our Lord bless you and your family the faith to know of God's grace, your Savior is born. Amen.

12/18/2020 – *The Christmas Story – Part 6* – Luke 2:8

Luke 2:8

> 8 And in the same region there were shepherds out in the field, keeping watch over their flock by night. (ESV)

And in the same region there were shepherds out in the field, keeping watch over their flock by night.

Bethlehem, where Jesus was born, lies about six miles south of Jerusalem. In the hills around the city of David, shepherds had been tending flocks for several thousand years before our Savior's birth. Even David, the king from whom Jesus was descended, began as a shepherd.

Of course we don't know the identity of the shepherds, nor the owners of the sheep. Many people speculate that the shepherds were in the employment of the Temple, caring for the animals used for the daily sacrifices. Just the two daily sacrifices, morning and evening, required over 720 lambs without spot or blemish. Add the animals purchased at the Temple for the other sacrifices, and we can see there is a need for very large flocks.

Could the shepherds have been tending the very lambs which pointed to the ultimate sacrifice of God's Son, called by John the Baptist the "Lamb of God?" There would be no more fitting group of people to hear of the Savior's birth, to know the thrill of meeting the parents of the Holy Child, the parents who tended Mary's offspring with the same tender care of the shepherds tending a new-born lamb.

May our Lord bless you and your family the faith to know of God's grace, Jesus' birth is for your blessing. Amen.

12/21/2020 – *The Christmas Story* – Part 7 – Luke 2:9

Luke 2:9

> 9 And an angel of the Lord appeared to them, and the glory of the Lord shone around them, and they were filled with fear. (ESV)

> And an angel of the Lord appeared to them, and the glory of the Lord shone around them, and they were filled with fear.

Very few people doubt the existence of angels. From the earliest chapters of Genesis, where God placed an angel to guard the tree of life in the Garden of Eden to the last chapters of Revelation, the Bible is filled with stories of these messengers of God. Although we do not know exactly when these spiritual beings were created, we do know they are very powerful and formidable.

The name "angel" means "messenger, or one sent." Although we think of the winged cherubim and seraphim as angels, the Bible occasionally uses the term for any messenger of God, such as a pastor. We may not recognize the angels who tell us of God's love, but those who speak of His grace bring us the good news of our salvation.

If we suspect that the shepherds near Bethlehem saw cute angels such as depicted on many Christmas cards, we would be sadly mistaken. Not only was their arrival frightening, but they reflected the full glory and majesty of the One who sent them. Is it any wonder that the shepherds were afraid?

May our Lord bless you and your family with the message of hope found in Infant of Bethlehem. Amen.

12/22/2020 – *The Christmas Story* – Part 8 – Luke 2:10–12

Luke 2:10–12

> 9 And the angel said to them, "Fear not, for behold, I bring you good news of a great joy that will be for all the people.
>
> 11 For unto you is born this day in the city of David a Savior, who is Christ the Lord.
>
> 12 And this will be a sign for you: you will find a baby wrapped in swaddling cloths and lying in a manger." (ESV)

>> And the angel said to them, "Fear not, for behold, I bring you good news of a great joy that will be for all the people. For unto you is born this day in the city of David a Savior, who is Christ the Lord. And this will be a sign for you: you will find a baby wrapped in swaddling cloths and lying in a manger."

We can spend a lifetime pondering this wonderful news and not begin to understand everything it means. The Son of God has taken upon Himself our human flesh. He, through whom all things were made, lies helplessly in a manger, true man in every respect except for the taint of inherited sin.

"Fear not," the angel said. Of course, this was to calm the frightened shepherds, startled by the bright light shining in the Judean darkness. More-so, it is the proclamation that we need not fear sin nor death, for the Savior has been born who will defeat Satan and the grave. God, in the fullness of time, acted on behalf of all mankind.

Do you wish to see how God works, how He brings His love to us? It is not through some nebulous philosophy, but through things which we can see, touch, and hear. The shepherds were not directed to look at their hearts or emotions, but to seek a baby lying in a manger. This news was accompanied with physical signs, in a place and at a time for which we have witnesses. This baby is Christ the Lord, one who can be found, one who comes to us.

May our Lord bless you and your family with the good news that the Son of God took on our humanity for our salvation. Amen.

12/23/2020 – *The Christmas Story* – Part 9 – Luke 2:13–14

Luke 2:13–14

> 13 And suddenly there was with the angel a multitude of the heavenly host praising God and saying,
>
> 14 Glory to God in the highest, and on earth peace among those with whom he is pleased! (ESV)

> And suddenly there was with the angel a multitude of the heavenly host praising God and saying, "Glory to God in the highest, and on earth peace among those with whom he is pleased!"

Upon the announcement of the birth of our Savior, all the heavenly hosts burst into song. They could not contain their joy, for God has truly redeemed His people. The shepherds could only listen in shock and awe as countless angels proclaimed God's love and mercy.

All glory goes to God for our salvation. We cannot, by our own reason or strength, believe in Jesus Christ or come to faith in Him. The Holy Spirit calls us to faith through the proclaimed Word of God and through the sacraments which physically bring us the forgiveness won for us by Jesus. Our Creator desires that we be and remain with Him, now and forever. May His will that all people be saved and come to the knowledge of the truth be done.

May our Lord bless you and your family with the good news that God gives us the forgiveness of our sins because of His love. Amen.

12/24/2020 – *The Christmas Story – Part 10* – Luke 2:13–14

Luke 2:13–14

> 13 And suddenly there was with the angel a multitude of the heavenly host praising God and saying,
>
> 14 Glory to God in the highest, and on earth peace among those with whom he is pleased! (ESV)

>> And suddenly there was with the angel a multitude of the heavenly host praising God and saying, "Glory to God in the highest, and on earth peace among those with whom he is pleased!"

What is the peace which the angel messengers announced to the shepherds? Is it the end of all wars and violence? Eventually, for this world will come to an end. Yet while there are sinful people, and all people are sinful, we shall have strife and conflict. Is it forced silence because of fear, such as we saw during the Cold War when both the United States and the Soviet Union were afraid of all-out conflict? No, for fear does not bring comfort, though fear may produce a sort of safety.

The peace which is yours in Christ Jesus this day, the peace of being reconciled with the Father, the peace of knowing that you have eternal life, comes from the forgiveness of sins. That forgiveness, for the sake of Jesus' suffering, death, and resurrection, is complete. You and I can add nothing to earn the forgiveness of our sins. We are declared holy and righteous in God's sight.

Saint Paul wrote, "For the wages of sin is death, but the free gift of God is eternal life in Christ Jesus our Lord."[58] Romans 6:23 Because you are declared sinless in God's sight, you have the hope of eternal life. That is the true peace which passes all understanding.

May our Lord bless you and your family with the good news that God gives you His peace. Amen.

---

[58] Romans 6:23 (ESV)

12/25/2020 – *The Christmas Story* – Part 11 – Luke 2:13–14

Luke 2:13–14

> 13 And suddenly there was with the angel a multitude of the heavenly host praising God and saying,
>
> 14 Glory to God in the highest, and on earth peace among those with whom he is pleased! (ESV)

> And suddenly there was with the angel a multitude of the heavenly host praising God and saying, "Glory to God in the highest, and on earth peace among those with whom he is pleased!"

On the sixth day of creation, God declared that His creation, including mankind, was "very good." He was pleased with Adam and Eve, and was happy with the outcome of all His creative work. Unfortunately, Adam desired to take God's glory for himself, succumbing, as did Eve, to the temptation to "become like God" by eating of the fruit of the Tree of the Knowledge of Good and Evil.

Immediately God, who could have destroyed all of creation, promised a Savior who would crush the head of Satan. The victory of sin would be costly, but our Heavenly Father loved His creation so much that even the sacrifice of His only-begotten Son would not be too high a price for their redemption.

Thus, the older rendering of the angels' song may be best. "Glory to God in the highest, and peace, goodwill towards men." The goodwill that God gives is the gift of forgiveness won by the Infant who was born in Bethlehem.

May our Lord bless you and your family with the good news that God is pleased to give us His mercy. Amen.

12/28/2020 – *The Christmas Story* – Part 12 – Luke 2:15

Luke 2:15

> 15 When the angels went away from them into heaven, the shepherds said to one another, "Let us go over to Bethlehem and see this thing that has happened, which the Lord has made known to us." (ESV)

> When the angels went away from them into heaven, the shepherds said to one another, "Let us go over to Bethlehem and see this thing that has happened, which the Lord has made known to us."

Saint Paul wrote, in his epistle to Rome: "So faith comes from hearing, and hearing through the word of Christ."[59] Romans 10:17 We are constantly bombarded with messages, most of which we ignore. Because the human mind can process only a finite amount of information, we tend to focus on that which is important at the time, filtering out other sights and sounds.

First, the angel host needed to get the attention of the shepherds. A bright light and heavenly chorus accomplished this nicely. Next they needed to speak of something important. "To you is born this day in the city of David a Savior who is Christ the Lord," piqued their curiosity.

When confronted with a life-changing truth, we respond. So the shepherds consulted together and decided to act on the angelic message. They went to Bethlehem. How could they have done anything less?

"To you is born this day in the city of David a Savior who is Christ the Lord." You also have the opportunity to respond. Will you, too, go to Bethlehem?

May our Lord bless you and your family with the desire to learn more of God's grace and mercy. Amen.

---

[59] Romans 10:17 (ESV)

12/29/2020 – *The Christmas Story – Part 13* – Luke 2:16

Luke 2:16

> 16 And they went with haste and found Mary and Joseph, and the baby lying in a manger. (ESV)

> And they went with haste and found Mary and Joseph, and the baby lying in a manger.

We have all seen the jokes about the sleazy used-car salesman who exaggerates when describing the condition of the vehicle he is trying to sell. "Buyer beware" is the watchword of the day. Others may be more generous, saying, "Trust, but verify."

The shepherds heard the angel proclamation. They could have stayed around their warm fire, discussing that they guessed the angels were telling the truth. Or they could leave their flocks and see for themselves.

Trust, but verify, was their watchword. Lo and behold, the angel was right, there was a baby lying in the manger, wrapped in swaddling clothes. The details checked out, the angel's message was true.

Today you hear, "For unto you is born this day in the city of David a Savior, who is Christ the Lord." Are we going to sit by the warm fire and take the messenger's word, or are we going to trust, but verify? What evidence do you need to see that God's Word, the Bible, is true? How will you investigate the story of God's love?

May our Lord bless you and your family with the certain knowledge His Word is true. Amen.

12/30/2020 – *The Christmas Story – Part 14* – Luke 2:17

Luke 2:17

> 17 And when they saw it, they made known the saying that had been told them concerning this child. (ESV)
>
>> And when they saw it, they made known the saying that had been told them concerning this child.

In the days when the telephone company had switchboards and operators, extra people were scheduled for Christmas day. The switchboard would light up with people trying to call friends and family to tell of their good fortune, to speak of their presents, to share the joy of the day. When something good happens, we tell others.

Although the shepherds lived over 2,000 years ago, they were just like you and me. They had news, they wanted to talk. Everyone they met heard their story of the angel message. They repeated the hymn, "Glory to God in the highest." They described the manger and the baby and spoke of their shock at hearing of the birth of the Messiah, the Savior.

As the days went on, the shepherds spoke of other things, but never forgot the angelic host. On occasion they would say to one another, "Do you remember that night?" The story was passed from shepherd to shepherd until a physician, Luke, wrote it down for all the world to hear.

What will you do with this message, "For unto you is born this day in the city of David a Savior, who is Christ the Lord?" Will you find the awe and wonder that God loves you so much as to sacrifice His only-begotten Son on your behalf?

May our Lord bless you and your family with the opportunities to share the good news of Jesus' birth. Amen.

12/31/2020 – *The Christmas Story* – Part 15 – Luke 2:18–20

Luke 2:18–20

> 17 And all who heard it wondered at what the shepherds told them.
>
> 19 But Mary treasured up all these things, pondering them in her heart.
>
> 20 And the shepherds returned, glorifying and praising God for all they had heard and seen, as it had been told them. (ESV)

>> And all who heard it wondered at what the shepherds told them.
>> But Mary treasured up all these things, pondering them in her heart.
>> And the shepherds returned, glorifying and praising God for all they had heard and seen, as it had been told them.

What are we going to do with the news that the shepherds told, that they saw the baby Jesus as the angel said? We can't remain neutral.

Many of the people in Bethlehem marveled at the story. It had all the trappings of a good adventure. Did they believe it? Did they care? Certainly some did, but probably many, like the forty percent of Americans who claim no religion, could not be bothered to investigate.

Mary, Jesus' mother, certainly knew that her Son was in incarnate Messiah. She thought about this, she looked for the meaning of this, she trusted God because of His message. Thus we, like Mary, also read, learn, study, and ponder the wonder of God's undeserved love and mercy. We hold fast to the promise of the forgiveness of sins for the sake of the death and resurrection of the Infant of Bethlehem.

Like the shepherds, we praise God for His mercy, for revealing to us His plan for our redemption from sin, death, and the power of the devil.

May our Lord bless you and your family as you contemplate Jesus' birth. Amen.

01/01/2021 – *The Christmas Story – Part 16* – Luke 2:11

Luke 2:11

> 11 For unto you is born this day in the city of David a Savior, who is Christ the Lord. (ESV)

> For unto you is born this day in the city of David a Savior, who is Christ the Lord.

We have come to the end of the story. Let's leave with the words of the first president of the Lutheran Church – Missouri Synod, the church body to which Trinity Lutheran Church belongs. Dr. Carl Ferdinand Walther wrote:

> What happened in Bethlehem was the fulfillment of that eternal decree of the heavenly father. As soon as His Son became man, the unbearable burden of all humanity's sin was laid upon Him. And so, as Christ, God's sacrificial Lamb for the sins of the whole world, lay in a hard crib in a dark stable, the eyes of God looked into the future to see His Son already dying on the cross. Therefore, this atonement for sins, by which God's offended holiness and righteousness were satisfied and men were reconciled to Him, was already accomplished.[60]

May our Lord bless you and your family. Amen.

---

[60] Quoted in *Treasure of Daily Prayer*, p. 1046

Index

Genesis
  2
    18 117
Exodus
  3
    13 19
  20
    3 .... 34, 98–100
    4–6 101
    5b–6 133
    7 103–105
    8 106–109
    12 110–114
    13 .... 115, 116
    14 .... 117, 118
    15 119–123
    16 .... 124, 125, 128–130
    17 .... 131, 132
Psalms
  23
    1 12–14
    2 .... 15, 16
    3 17–19
    4 .... 20, 21
    5 22–24
    6 25
  34
    8 15
  42
    2 79
  50
    15 36
  119
    105 .... 136, 137
Proverbs
  6
    23 97
  11
    1 121
Isaiah
  9
    6 .... 19, 37
    7 140
  55
    1 79
  64
    6 97
Matthew
  5
    3 .... 72, 73
    4 .... 74, 75
    5 .... 76, 77
    6 .... 78, 79
    7 80–83
    8 .... 84, 85
    9 86
    10 87–89
    11–12 .... 90, 91
    21–22 116
    27–28 131
  6
    9 32–39

10	40–44
11	45–47
12	48–51
13	52–61
33	62, 67–71

18
- 15–17 130

22
- 37–39 136

Luke

2
- 1–3 .... 138, 139
- 4–5 .... 140, 141
- 6–7 142
- 8 143
- 9 144
- 10–12 145
- 11 153
- 13–14 146–148
- 15 149
- 16 150
- 17 151
- 18–20 152

10
- 27 93

11
- 1 26

John

3
- 16 12

4
- 7–26 79

10
- 14 12

15
- 18–19 88

20
- 30–31 5

Romans

3
- 20 135

5
- 1–5 3

6
- 3–4 9–11
- 23 .... 75, 147

8
- 3–4 92

10
- 9 .... 7, 8
- 17 149

13
- 3–4 134

Galatians

3
- 26 32

Colossians

3
- 17 62–66

Titus

1
- 15 85

Hebrews

11
- 1 2

James

3
- 6–8 129

1 Corinthians

1
- 23 .... 1, 8

1 John

1
- 10 .... 95, 96

2
- 1 35

3
- 1 32

1 Thessalonians

4
- 13 74

5
- 16–18 27–31

1 Timothy

1
- 9–10 94

2
- 1–4 126
- 4 42

2 Timothy

4
- 2 6

Made in the USA
Monee, IL
11 June 2022